If God already knows,

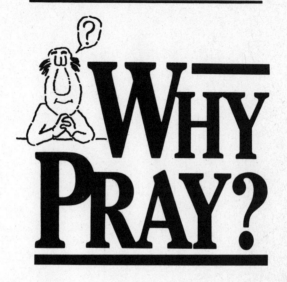

WHY PRAY?

If God already knows,

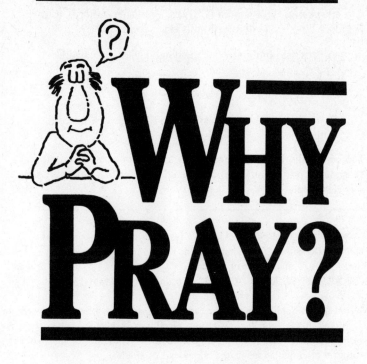

WHY PRAY?

Douglas F. Kelly, Ph.D.
with Caroline S. Kelly

Wolgemuth & Hyatt, Publishers, Inc.
Brentwood, Tennessee

The mission of Wolgemuth & Hyatt, Publishers, Inc. is to publish and distribute books that lead individuals toward:

- A personal faith in the one true God: Father, Son, and Holy Spirit;

- A lifestyle of practical discipleship; and

- A worldview that is consistent with the historic, Christian faith.

Moreover, the Company endeavors to accomplish this mission at a reasonable profit and in a manner which glorifies God and serves His Kingdom.

© 1989 by Douglas F. Kelly. All rights reserved
Published December 1989. First Edition
Printed in the United States of America
96 95 94 93 92 91 90   8 7 6 5 4 3 2 (Second printing, May 1990)

Unless otherwise noted, all scripture quotations are from the New King James Version of the Bible, © 1979, 1980, 1982, 1984 by Thomas Nelson, Inc., Nashville, Tennessee and are used by permission.

Wolgemuth & Hyatt, Publishers, Inc.
1749 Mallory Lane, Suite 110, Brentwood, Tennessee 37027.

Library of Congress Cataloging-in-Publication Data

Kelly, Douglas F.
    If God already knows, why pray? / Douglas F. Kelly. — 1st ed.
        p. cm
    ISBN 0-943497-76-0
    1. Prayer. 2. Providence and government of God.   I. Title.
BV210.2.K38 1989
248.3'2 — dc20   89-39030
                                                          CIP

To Caroline Anne Frances Switzer Kelly,
beloved wife, fellow pilgrim, wonderful helper,
whose *yes* to me was an answer to two years of prayer.

CONTENTS

ACKNOWLEDGMENTS

These thoughts on prayer were drawn together in preparation for various lectures delivered over a twelve-month period, first at Pensacola Theological Institute in McIlwaine Memorial Presbyterian Church in Pensacola, Florida in July 1987. Later the same topics were addressed at several locations in Scotland during Rutherford House Week, May 1988, as well as at the inauguration of the Thomas Charles Institute of the Evangelical Movement of Wales at Bridgend in June 1988.

From early childhood in my parents' home in Lumberton, North Carolina (where my mother's mother, Ruth Parker Pate, also lived), as well as in the homes of my father's Aunt Mamie (Blue Britt) in Pembroke, North Carolina and his Aunt Maude (Blue Hendren) in Moore County, North Carolina, I lived and visited where believing prayer was the daily atmosphere. But there are others who have influenced me deeply. I am especially grateful for the life of Miss Flora A. Fraser (born on the Isle of Skye in 1889, died in Edinburgh in 1973). More perhaps than any other single person, she showed me (without knowing she was doing so) what a life of prayer is like. And I remember with great appreciation my late cousin, Mrs. Neilina Kelly Scott of Heaste, Isle of Skye (1894–

1983), whose almost constant intercession for us supported us through many crises.

I would also like to express my appreciation to the prayer meetings of Holyrood Abbey Church of Scotland, Edinburgh, and its minister, The Rev. James Philip; to that of Gilcomston South Church of Scotland, Aberdeen, and its minister, The Rev. William Still; as well as to that of St. Columba's Free Church of Scotland, Edinburgh, and its (now retired) minister, The Rev. Donald Lamont. Each of these showed me, during my formative student years, exactly what a faithful congregational prayer meeting can be and do. And I thank them for prayer support in the years since then.

As far as the actual publication of the material as a book is concerned, I am grateful for encouragement from Dr. Luder Whitlock and Mr. Lyn Perez of Reformed Theological Seminary in Jackson, Mississippi, and Orlando, Florida. I appreciate the proofreading and other assistance with this book from my students and friends, Duncan Rankin, John Farrar, Tito Padilla, John Koelling, Jon Balserak, Bill Moore, Steve Froehlich, Jeff Moes, Bill Thrailkill, Richard Thomas, Joey Stewart, Celia Wood, and Knox Chamblin as well as the good help of my secretary, Mrs. Mary Atwood of Jackson. In addition, thanks are due to Dr. Nigel Cameron, Miss Janella Glover, and others of the staff of Rutherford House for their help while I was working through this volume in 1988 in Edinburgh. And I especially thank Dr. Frank Gibson, Chairman of the Church of Scotland Board of Social Responsibility, for great help during our stays in Scotland. I appreciate the permission of Baker Book House to make reference to the fine volume by Dick Eastman, *The Hour That Changes the World*. I have also benefited a great deal from *The Theology of Prayer* by Dr. B. M. Palmer, who was Minister of First Presbyterian Church of New Orleans during much of the nineteenth century.

Special thanks to several friends who helped close our house and pack our belongings while I was busy with final preparation for much of this material during the last week of July 1987. In particular, I thank Robert Lucas of Greenwood, Mississippi, and the following from Dillon, South Carolina: Coble Adams, Jim and Robin Atkins, Sally McRae Bennett, Shannon Bethea, The Rev. John Bumgardner, John Hugh and Belle Campbell, Curtis DuBose, Willy and Virginia Hobeika, and Bill and Frances McNeill, as well as Blandine Madinier, our nanny from Lyon, and her predecessor, Pierina Sandoz of Paris. In addition, I wish to express thanks to our children, Douglas II, Martha, Angus, Daniel, and Patrick for their patience and the way they often managed routine chores without Caroline's or my help while we were both immersed in the final revisions.

Above all others, I am most grateful to my dear wife, Caroline, who has massively improved this volume by thoroughly working through its entirety in order to change it from a largely spoken form to a more readable written form. Once again I have cause to be full of praise that Proverbs 18:22 is true in my own experience.

Finally, if God in Christ were not absolutely real and wonderfully forgiving and gracious, and if He had not constantly been answering my prayers since I was four or five years old, you can be sure I would never have bothered to write this book.

Douglas F. Kelly
Edinburgh
June 1989

INTRODUCTION

P rayer changes the world: it makes good things happen because it gets God's will done and thus brings down His best blessings. This is the message of the Old and New Testaments, as well as the experience of God's people throughout the ages. The God of the Scriptures has great blessings stored up for His people, but He has so planned it that those blessings can only be released by the prayers of His people.

The power of prayer to change things by bringing into one's life good things (which are later seen to have been part of the eternal plan of God) is illustrated in a rather unusual romance. In 1970 an American postgraduate student from the southern states was captivated by the beauty, intelligence, and faith of an English girl who was studying, as he was, at the University of Edinburgh.

Instead of asking the attractive girl out on dates, the rather quiet southern boy started praying hard that the Lord would prepare the girl to marry him! He prayed constantly for two years, at times beginning to wonder if he were trying to force the Lord into something that perhaps only he, rather than the Lord, wanted. And all during this time the girl showed few, if any, signs of interest — or even disinterest! Yet the lad prayed on, and one day popped the question, which to his delight was answered with a definite yes.

But had he actually forced the Lord's hand? As the years passed and children were born and the parents engaged in Christian ministry, there was more and more evidence — in small as well as in large ways — that they were truly meant for each other; that they made a team intellectually, spiritually, culturally, as well as physically and family-wise. Only God could have brought them together.

Therefore, the student's two years of constant praying, instead of getting God to do something He was hesitant to do, actually released the blessings of a partnership the Lord had planned from eternity. God made the plan and then used the prayers to bring His plan into happy execution.

The principle is clear: the seeking of God in prayer releases the blessing of God.

This truth is expressed very well for us in a book written by the Norwegian theologian, O. Hallesby, entitled simply, *Prayer*.[1] He said that the essence of prayer is opening the door of our lives to the risen Christ. In other words, what we are really doing in prayer is asking Him to come into our human situation, with all our many needs, and flood even our spiritual deadness with His resurrection power. This is precisely what the risen Lord is talking about in Revelation 3:20, "Behold, I stand at the door and knock. If anyone . . . opens the door, I will come in to him and dine with him, and he with Me."

My hope is that these brief studies on the meaning of prayer will be just that — an opening for the risen Lord Jesus Christ to invade your life and the thousand situations which burden your heart. Then you, and those for whom you are burdened, will be empowered with His resurrec-

tion life and glory. That is what you and I desperately
need every day.

Not Just Theory or Technique

Being intellectual about prayer is too easy. We so often
concern ourselves with the technique or the theory or the
dry theology of prayer for its own sake. In fact, we listen
to and even discuss and store away information without
allowing it to affect our behavior.

When we lived in Scotland, we were once arranging
for one of our sons to travel by train to another town to
spend a few days with friends. The night before he was
due to leave, we were watching the evening news on the
TV and discussing the reports of railroad strikes planned
for each Wednesday of that month. We were even specu-
lating as to how long the Unions would continue with this
action before some agreement could be reached.

The next day, my wife and our son went downtown to
the station. It was deserted — not a train in sight! Eventually they found a small chalkboard announcing that since it
was Wednesday, no trains would be running. Now, both of
them could both have repeated the information that had
been on the news, but it had made absolutely no impact on
their behavior!

This can so often be true with the subject of prayer.
We discuss and debate the issue and then actually fail to
seek the face of God. As a professor of theology, I know
how strong that temptation can be! Intellectual pride can
sometimes keep the door of our lives closed fast to the
reality of the glory and power of Christ's disturbing, but
ultimately uplifting presence. Let us be aware of this
harmful temptation. Dr. James I. Packer recently remarked,

"[The] most crucial problem I have found in these communities over the years . . . is [how] to make our theology serve our godliness; to make theological education advance our Christian discipleship."

He was wise to the dangers of theorizing because students would sometimes tell him at the end of a theology course, "God is not so real to me now as He was when I started. Though I know more about Him, He seems now more distant to me, and I am less excited about Him than I was." Packer wisely says, "When a student speaks like that, his theology and his discipleship have been disconnected."[2]

We should make sure that our theology and our discipleship are thoroughly connected so that we can be more godly, praying, and prevailing men and women of the Cross, the empty tomb, and the power-filled heavenly throne! Thus we seek to understand what the Bible teaches about the meaning of prayer in a way that will inform our minds, warm our hearts, and move our wills.

True Prayer

What could be better, if we desire to understand and act upon the meaning of prayer, than to sit at the feet of Jesus, our great High Priest. Now, what is the value of having Jesus as a priest? That is what he is called in the Bible, but what exactly is a priest? What does a priest do?

The priest represents the people before the altar. He offers the sacrifices, and it is he who offers the prayers on behalf of the people.

Jesus, as our Great High Priest, represents us before the heavenly altar. He has permanently opened the way to God for us through the sacrifice of his *own* body, so that we have the assurance of direct access to God when we pray. And He continually prays for us.

We do not have to go to church, or have someone who is ordained pray for us in order to have our prayer heard. We can go through Jesus, who is still a priest in heaven, praying even now for his people. He is the one, above all, who knows how to pray, whose prayers are effective. And he it is who gave us that most perfect form of prayer, "The Lord's Prayer."

Thus the first chapters of this book are deliberately based upon that prayer. By looking at the structure of this divine formula, we should be able to discern the very heart of the Biblical theology of prayer.

Although we will look at some of the specific petitions of the prayer in detail, that is not our primary goal. Rather we want to get to the root of what prayer really is, and use the Lord's Prayer as much as possible to help us do this.

We will discover that the various sections of the Lord's Prayer are like powerful magnets which draw together in orderly fashion all the separate multitude of prayer texts scattered throughout the Scriptures.

This prayer is in the sixth chapter of Matthew as well as the eleventh chapter of Luke. Now, Matthew 6 is a part of the larger context of the Sermon on the Mount, and in this section, Jesus deals with three distinct expressions of the religious life as they were summarized in Judaism.

In the first verses He warns His disciples against doing "alms" (KJV), "charitable deeds" (NKJV), or "acts of righteousness" (NIV) before men with the wrong motive. From verses 5 through 15 He warns about praying as the hypocrites do, and then at verse 16, He raises the question of fasting. Thus almsgiving, praying, and fasting are the focus of our Lord's teaching here.

Probably He has in mind the way the Pharisees of His day had perverted the religious life from something that was good, beautiful, and true into an externalized and harsh system of religion which actually drove people away from God rather than toward Him. So He is actually not only dealing with those three major points but also with how those points had been corrupted by the Pharisaic interpretation of religion in His time.

The reward of the Pharisees was that they were seen of men. Ironically, our Lord is saying their prayers will be answered, but since they are only praying with the desire to be seen of men and to be thought of as praying men, then their prayer is answered, and they have their reward on earth and earth only. They have made no impact for eternity.

In verse 7 Jesus says the heathen think they shall be heard for their "vain repetitions." Well, if they were not heard for their vain repetitions (and Jesus says they were not), then what are we heard for when we pray? The answer to this is in the Lord's Prayer.

God First

Have you ever been in a church which has somewhere on the walls a representation of the stone tablets on which God wrote the Ten Commandments? Usually the first tablet lists the first four, and the last six are on the second, illustrating that the first relates to God and the second relates to man. Thus, God is first and man is second, which is the only right approach to the meaning of life.

In exactly the same way, we can divide the Lord's Prayer into two basic sections. The first section, Matthew 6:9-10, deals with God: "Our Father in heaven, hallowed be Your name. Your kingdom come. Your will be done on earth as it is in heaven."

The second section of the Lord's Prayer deals with manward realities and human considerations, which also have a legitimate, though secondary, place: daily bread, debts, and temptation.

Perhaps we could say that the Lord's Prayer is really a variation and an exposition of verse 33 of Matthew 6, "But seek first the kingdom of God and His righteousness, and all these things shall be added to you." In other words, the first half of the Lord's Prayer deals with the kingdom of God and its righteousness and the second half of the prayer deals with "all these things" which shall be added to us: the pardon, the provision, and the protection.

Significantly Jesus says "do not worry about tomorrow for. . . sufficient for the day is its own trouble" (v. 34). In other words, if we can get the first part of the prayer right, then the second part of the prayer will surely follow. If we get the will of God, the kingdom of God, and the hallowing of God's name right, then we will be all the surer of having the second part of the prayer answered when we pray, "Give us this day our daily bread."

The Humanistic Lie

Let me say here that the Lord's Prayer and the Ten Commandments, Matthew 6:33 and Genesis 1:1 and the whole Bible, are totally opposed to the spirit of the age in which you and I have been called by God to live. We live in an age when secular humanism is dominant. We simply do not think first of God when we face difficulty. On a lighter vein, this kind of attitude is reflected in the story of a nervous passenger in the days when people traveled to Europe by ship.

As a serious storm was threatening the vessel, she grabbed the Captain wailing. "This is terrifying. Is there anything I can do to help?"

"Well, you can always pray," answered the Captain.

"Oh no," she cried. "Is it as bad as that!"

This may be a humorous story, but most of us can identify with the sentiment. God, if He exists, is simply a last resort.

This kind of reasoning is most evident in *Humanist Manifesto I* of 1933 and *Humanist Manifesto II* of 1973. Those secularist thinkers, who influence so much of our modern culture, believe that man and not God should be first. Indeed, they wish to exclude God completely. They feel that the idea of God is very harmful and dangerous to our evolutionary progress.

Such "man first" and "man only" thinking has caused God and Christianity to be increasingly excluded from modern culture and especially from our school systems. For example, the 1987 Public School Textbook Case in Mobile, Alabama, impressively demonstrated the systematic exclusion of any serious reference to God or to the influence of Christianity in both European and American history. It argued that humanism had become a substitute religion for Christianity and had excluded the Biblical point of view from textbooks.

For example, many school texts have replaced the designation, B.C. with the initials, B.C.E., when referring to dates. Rather than directly refer to the birth of Christ as the starting point for historical dating in the West, they have introduced the phrase "Common Era", to eliminate the historical reference to Christ. Seen from that perspective, Christianity is presented as basically a social phenomenon, a temporary religious movement, rather than the turning point of history.

So our culture disposes us to put man first and then either to deny God or at the very least relegate Him to an inferior, unimportant status or to a last resort. The Pharisees did the same thing in a different way. They acted as though what people thought of them in the community was the final reality, whereas Jesus showed that was not the case at all. What matters is how we stand with God.

If we are aware of this man-centered tendency of our modern society, it will alert us to how radically different Biblical prayer is from the normal approach to life these days. To get our thinking and our praying in tune with the Spirit of Christ, we must ask the Holy Spirit to help us stretch our minds. Only then can we be lifted by faith above the oppressive, humanistic atmosphere with its basic premise that the only thing that is real is that which is material. When we think only in terms of what we can see and understand, we lack categories that recognize the supernatural, and thus miss some of the answers to our prayers.

A God Who Hears

When our oldest son was born, he was legally blind in one eye. With treatment over the years his eye has become fairly functional, if he is wearing glasses. However, when he was in seventh grade, the other eye, his good one, was hit by a racquetball. All of a sudden we faced the prospect of our son's vision in both eyes being seriously and permanently impaired.

For a few days he was out of school and could hardly watch TV, much less comfortably read a book. We alerted many friends and prayer meetings to pray for him. There was even a group of inmates praying in a local jail! When his sight did not improve much after the swelling had receded, it was time to have a specialist run some tests.

His mother took him to the office, where the technician ran a routine eye exam with an eye chart. Then dye was injected into the bloodstream to facilitate taking special pictures of the retina. Finally the specialist arrived to interpret the results. Nothing seemed to be wrong! There was a little scarring, but that was all!

My wife was amazed and slightly embarrassed. "What were the results of the eye exam?" she asked.

"They were fine!"

"But yesterday, he could hardly see out of that eye! How could it happen so fast? People have been praying, but . . ."

"Sometimes," answered the doctor, "that is what will do the trick."

We had been praying for a miracle, but when it came, it was almost as though we did not have a way to recognize it. My wife had to ask herself, "How else would a miracle look, if not like this?" and fight back the inclination to give the sudden improvement a purely natural explanation.

We need to ask the Holy Spirit to convince us that materialism is the devil's lie in this generation to rob us of the greatest, sweetest, most powerful blessings of God for our lives. May the Holy Spirit use these studies on prayer to convince us that the living, triune God is the most important factor of all.

A New Perspective

From this point of view then, every true prayer is a trumpet against secularism and an opening of the door to the reality of the glory and power of the risen Christ to flood into our entire situation. The key to life's meaning and the key to true prayer is God first, mankind second.

Hence our studies in the theology of prayer will follow this pattern laid down for us by Jesus in the Lord's Prayer. These eight chapters will take us into the very heart of the Biblical theology of prayer. They are written in a way that will help us not only understand the truths, but also move us to trust, to praise, and to pray. And we will discover that, far from being dry or merely intellectual, theology can be a handmaiden leading us to confident action.

PART 1

IF GOD ALREADY
KNOWS

Our Father
which art in heaven,
(Matthew 6:9)

1

PRAYER DEPENDS
ON WHO GOD IS

If there is such a thing as "the secret of life" or "the key of life," surely it would be found in the teaching and work of Jesus, who is "the Way, the Truth and the Life." No one can take a serious look at His life and teaching without being struck by the absolute importance and constant centrality of God the Father to all Christ said and did. Without the slightest exaggeration, He could say: "My food is to do the will of Him who sent Me" (John 4:34); "I must work the works of Him who sent Me while it is day" (John 9:4); "I always do those things that please Him" (John 8:29).

When we come to the prayer He teaches us, we find exactly the same order of priorities. The God who is so crucially important to all that Jesus says and does, is the foundation, center, and goal of that prayer. In other words, Jesus' prayer as well as His life teaches us that the most important fact in all of the world is what God is like. Thus, when we begin to pray, our first question should be, "What is this God like to whom we pray?"

Who Is God?

This momentous question is answered in two ways at the very beginning of the Lord's Prayer, because the words *Our Father in heaven* give God a name and tell us some thing about Him. What God is really like determines everything else both in theology and in practice. The better you know God the more certain it is that you will pray to Him. Let me give you an illustration of this from my own childhood.

My mother tells me that when I was about two years old, and my father had just returned from World War II, they decided to take a short vacation at one of the North Carolina beaches. After about three days, my grandmother brought me on the bus to join them. She had me on her lap in the back seat of the bus, and in those days, the back windows could be opened by the passengers.

As the bus drove up to the little station at Carolina Beach, I recognized my parents who were waiting for us. In the hot summer weather, the window happened to be open. Suddenly, without a word's warning, I leaped out of the bus toward my parents. Fortunately for my good health, my mother was able to move quickly enough to catch me before I landed on the ground!

I do not remember this at all, but it does illustrate a very important point about prayer. The better we know what our Heavenly Father is like, the more we will readily leap into His arms in prayer. Of course with our limited human minds we can never fully describe or comprehend the Almighty God. And yet He has made Himself known to us in a way that we can truly — though never totally — grasp.

Jesus calls God "Our Father" and tells us that He is "in heaven." On the one hand, Christ teaches us that God is a *person*; in fact, God is a father. On the other hand, Christ tells us that God is in heaven, beyond this earth. He is not part of it, nor subject to its limitations, because He is in total control of everything — of all the galaxies yet undiscovered! He has all power; He is *infinite*.

God Is a Person, like Us

What does it mean to know that God is a person? Recently we were in Korea and had the privilege of visiting a world famous Buddhist temple. Did we get the impression that the gold-painted statues in the shrines, surrounded by flickering candles, were "persons"? Could they hear our prayers? Not at all! Why not? Because we knew that they could neither hear nor communicate with us. An idol, as the Scriptures so rightly point out, is nothing but a deaf and dumb block of wood or stone!

So how is the God to whom we pray different? When Jesus calls Him Father, we immediately see that here is one who by definition is related to others — His children. And that is the most central meaning of the word *person*: to be related to others.

This may be a new way of looking at the meaning of the word. Generally we define a person as someone who has a mind, who is able to think, who has affections or emotions, who is able to love, hate, to be jealous, to yearn, to care, to make choices and decisions, and to say yes and no. But what is the point of all these abilities? To enable us to relate to others.

Think about your day. From the time the alarm rings, you are always in relationships with others. You are someone's child, whether or not you talk to a parent that day. You may be someone's parent, or a husband or wife.

At work, you are a manager or a subordinate, a client or a boss; in the marketplace, a consumer or a supplier. Some of these relationships are, of course, more significant than others, but the point is that to be human is to be inescapably linked to others.

When we look at the meaning of the word *person* in this way, we see why loneliness is such a devastating experience. We all remember moments as children when the crowd seemed to have passed us by, and we sat alone on the playground. Or think of the pity we feel for those we know who are sick or elderly, shut in with nothing but their own thoughts, day in and day out.

These kinds of experiences tell us that a person is simply not equipped to be a "rugged individual" throughout life. As the poet said, "No man is an island." In fact, there is a sense in which a single solitary being is not really a person at all, because the whole point of being a person lies in having the ability to communicate and share in a relationship.

The best definition of *personhood*, therefore, involves relationship, especially when considering that the Bible says people are created in the image of God. And is God a single, solitary individual? Of course not! You see, God the Father has always been Father and thus has never been without a Son. Scripture also teaches us that the Holy Spirit is eternally part of the Godhead as well. That means that the one true God has always had other persons within His own life with whom He could share and communicate. Thus, from all eternity the real definition of a person involves a relationship, precisely because God created us in His own image.

God Is Infinite, unlike Us

So we are like God in that we are persons, created in His image, and thus different from the animals. We can understand a little of what it means to say that He is a person by understanding our own personhood. But there is another sense in which we are very different from God because, as we have already noticed, He is infinite.

Of course, the infinity of God is something that we are not able fully to understand or properly illustrate, but perhaps that is not such a great problem as may appear at first glance. Several years ago, a little boy from a Christian home was in the fifth grade in a school in East Tennessee. His schoolteacher was not a Christian and, indeed, was hostile toward Christianity. In fact, she rather enjoyed embarrassing those children who had faith in God.

Hoping to humiliate him, one day she said to the little fifth grader, "Why can't you explain to me who God is?" With remarkable wisdom the little boy replied, "If I could explain who God is I would have to be as big as He is." The boy was right. None of us are able to explain the infinity of God, but that does not at all mean that we cannot really know who He is.

Jesus has told us that our Father is in heaven, above everything. Another way of saying the same thing is that He is *transcendent* to everything. He is above all, He made all, and He is the source of all. When we say that He is infinite, we mean that He is completely unlimited. He is unlimited by space and time, because, after all, He made them both. We also know from Scripture that God has all power, and that there is no limitation to His wisdom, love, purity, and majesty. The God in heaven, to whom Jesus teaches us to pray, can view at a glance the entire stretch of history and already knows everything that will happen in the future.

How different from us! We are finite and subject to all kinds of limitations — mental, physical, and emotional. You and I exist as whole persons between our conception in the womb of our mother and our physical death. Each of us has a beginning and an end. Of course we have immortal souls that continue beyond physical death, but even these depend upon the God who was and is and always will be there.

Can the Gap Be Bridged?

Now because we limited humans are so different from the infinite God, some philosophers and theologians have decided that we cannot really know a God who is so far above us. How could we possibly talk to Him?

This false idea is one of the first principles of the Existentialist philosophy which was so influential in France — and in the whole intellectual world — after World War II. Indeed, the empty churches of modern Paris are a mute testimony. And, interestingly, the despair concerning personal relationships, that echoes through the writings of men such as Sartre and Camus, shows us how a loss of the knowledge that God is personal can affect man's view of himself.

But the first line of the Lord's Prayer helps us find the right balance. We can avoid the disastrous idea that we cannot know the infinite God, because here we are taught that He is personal, as well as infinite. Thus, although we do not understand infinity, if He is personal and I am personal, then it is most reasonable to believe that we can know each other. Furthermore, the most logical thing in all the world is that God would talk to us.

Within the heart of God, John 1:1 tells us, there is the *Word;* there is communication. "In the beginning was the *Word*" (emphasis added). There has always been language in God, communication and sharing within God Himself. And since God made us in His image, He made us so that He could share with us and talk to us. Therefore, to believe that God has spoken to the human race in words we can understand (namely, the Bible) should not seem at all surprising.

Why would He have gone to the trouble to create us in His image and then not say anything to us? To have a silent universe, where the Creator did not speak to His creatures, would be very strange indeed! But He has made us in His image and spoken to us in His Word and through His Son. Therefore, the most logical thing for us to do is to respond and talk back to Him in prayer.

Love within the Trinity

The Lord's Prayer has taught us that God is an infinite person. He is like us—a father is a person—but different—far above us and over all in heaven. We have already seen that a person is someone capable of relationships with others. When Jesus tells us that God is Father, He is telling us that in His inmost being He is involved in a relationship.

This is precisely the basis of the Christian doctrine of the Trinity: the God of Scripture is not just a single, solitary, lonely individual, but He is actually a *trinity* of persons. The word *trinity* comes from *tri* (three) + *unity.* He is one God, and only one God, but He exists in *three* persons: Father, Son, and Holy Ghost.

Of course, we have to admit that this is a mystery, passing any human explanation. However, though theologians cannot explain the Trinity, some of them have been able to shed some light on its meaning. Possibly the theologian who had the clearest insight into the Holy Trinity was a twelfth-century Scot named Richard, who lived in the Abbey of St. Victor near Paris. Thus he was known as Richard of St. Victor.

Richard wrote a wonderful book on the Trinity in which he asked the question: Why is God a Trinity rather than just a solitary, lonely individual? He said that it is because "God is Love," and the nature of love is to be overflowing and abundant and outgoing.[1] It takes more than one to share love, so God is not just one person but three.

If you are married, do you remember those first days when you realized that you were in love, and that this was the real thing? Do you remember discovering how easy it was to do little things for the other person, what a delight it was to share, and how your joy even overflowed into other relationships? Real love is never selfish or egocentric or turned inward but pours itself out and desires someone else with whom it may share its blessedness, its joy, and its sweetness—in a word, its life.

In the same way, God, having been Love from eternity, has always existed in three persons who can share in that love. Thus God has never been a single, atomistic individual but has ever lived the "family" existence of three in one (see Ephesians 3:14, 15).

Life, Light, and Love Overflowing from God

In the Gospel of John, the book of Revelation, and 1 John, we often find these words applied to God: light and life and love. "God is *light* and in Him is no darkness at all" (1 John 1:5, emphasis added). "I am the way, the truth, and the *life*" (John 14:6, emphasis added). "God is *love*" (1 John 4:8, emphasis added). At the heart of His personality, God is overflowing with these three qualities. But they are not just shared among the Father, Son, and Holy Spirit; they overflow to *us!*

This is the way that love shown between parents filters down to their children, giving them a sense of being loved. But what God offers us is far greater. Revelation 22:1 talks of "a pure river of *water of life*, clear as crystal, proceeding from the throne of God and of the Lamb" (emphasis added). From this wonderful, glorious, beautiful triune God, there is always flowing a river of living water, a river of light, a river of love.

At last, here is the answer to the question: what is God like? This is what the triune God is like: life, light, and love. That is the secret to this universe and the key to understanding everything that exists. "Our Father in heaven" may be one of the first phrases we chanted as toddlers, but those few words are the doorway to knowing the nature of the infinite, personal, triune God.

By taking a close look at just these few words, we have discovered where we can go for *light,* to enable us to understand and then find the way out of personal or moral dilemmas; for *life,* when all around us seems to be disintegrating; and for *love,* when our relationships are unsatisfactory.

Such texts of Scripture as Ephesians, chapters 1, 2, and 5 and John, chapters 3 and 17, give us a clue as to why God made this material world and put people in it, why God even let each one of us be born. The Father so loved the Son, with this kind of generous, outgoing love, that He

wanted to make a world and fill it with a race of people who
would be like His Son. His goal was that there should be
others who could share in the light, life, and love of the Son.

In other words, there is a sense in which Christians are
elevated to take part in the blessed trinitarian life! Of
course, people remain creatures throughout eternity and
never become divine, but nonetheless they are lifted up
into a love relationship with the life of God that is absolutely real. To have a relationship with Christ means to be
drawn into the kind of relationship of love that He has
with the Father. God did not need people, not at all! It is
simply that His is the kind of love that wants to be shared.
So He made a world: He created people in His image. Or
to put it another way, what would be the finest gift the
Father could give His Son? Would it not be a wonderful,
beautiful bride? So it is as though God made the world as
a stage and put humanity on it, out of which He could
prepare a bride to be with His Son.

Almost two thousand years ago, when the early Christians were struggling to make a place for themselves in a
hostile, pagan society, one of their writings, *The Shepherd
of Hermas*, encouraged them with this realization, that the
world really exists for the church.[2] In fact, the world and
humanity in general, as well as the vast sweep of history,
are all here to be a stage or a nursery for the development of
the bride of Christ. That puts a different perspective on life!

The Gap Is Bridged

Do you see how all of this relates so directly to prayer?
The Father gives the Son a bride, and because of the
bride's relationship to the Son, the Father is now also the
Father of the bride. The bride can get through to the Fa-

ther and can speak to the Father in prayer. That, in the truest sense, is what Jesus means when He addresses "Our Father in heaven." He is the Father of those who are related to the Son as His bride.

In one sense God is the father of everyone by virtue of their creation in His image. But the Lord's Prayer is in the context of redemption, and in the ultimate sense, as far as prayer and salvation and eternity are concerned, the heavenly Father is father only to those who are redeemed through His Son.

Sin has put us out of favor with the Father. That is why He sent the Son to be our "sin-bearer." Sin has turned God into our enemy and us into His enemy, so that we no longer naturally say, "Our Father in heaven." Instead, we turn and run from God which, of course, is exactly what our secular humanistic society is doing. So many people today do not say, "loving, heavenly Father" but rather try to find every excuse to avoid acknowledging His reality. You see this running and hiding on television and in the movies. You may hear it in the schools, certainly in the universities. You sometimes even hear it in pulpits.

For example, why do you think that the theory of evolution enjoys such enormous support, when even secular scientists in many different universities are putting serious question marks against some of its basic assertions? Is it not that the only alternative is to postulate some kind of Creator God? And if there really is a God, then man is not supreme — a truth which is immensely threatening to many in our day.

Surely the rampant spread of sexually transmitted diseases in our culture is directly related to a deliberate disregard of traditional moral standards. As people cease to acknowledge the existence of any God, they lose an objective basis for defining right and wrong. So they imagine that they can redefine sexual morality according to their personal preference. The amazing thing is that anyone would rather run enormous risks to their health, and even to their life, than face the fact that God is real and His way is best!

But the heavenly Father is father to those who have laid down their weapons of rebellion against Him. This can only happen through the grace of Christ coming into their lives, waking them up, and opening their eyes to see the wonderful, glorious God and the beauty of salvation through His Son. As a result, they can become intimately related to the Son, as personal Lord and Savior. Then, and only then, will they begin to cry out *"Our* Father in heaven."

In the introduction, we noted the difference in the Sermon on the Mount between true and false praying. The Pharisees had their reward here on earth for their superficial religiosity. Once Christ even said to the Pharisees, "You are of your father, the devil." That is what we have to say to so much of our culture today, although we must say it with greatest humility and sadness: "You are of your father, the devil."

But there is good news for our humanistic culture, for as John 1:12 states: "But as many as received Him, to them He gave the right to become children of God." God becomes our heavenly Father through our union with Christ in the new birth by faith, which the Holy Spirit creates within us. In other words, though the book of Revelation tells us that in God's ultimate purposes, the consummation of the marriage of the church of Christ will be in heaven, we do not need to wait until then to enjoy an intimate relationship with Him. John 1:12 and other passages teach us that our relationship is not just that of in-law kinship, but of adoptive children.

Children Talk!

We are given some help by the Apostle Paul in Romans 8:14–17 and Galatians 4:4–7 in understanding why only the redeemed can really pray, "Our Father, in heaven." In the new birth, the Holy Spirit gives us the spirit of adoption, "by whom we cry out, 'Abba Father.'" *Abba* literally means something like *daddy* or *papa*, or some intimate term of endearment. We can use it because not only was the church as a whole destined to be the bride of His Son, but our own individual relationship to God changes. Through the forgiveness of our sins, we can finally become intimately related to Him; we become His children.

An interesting illustration of this secret work of the Spirit is found in an observation made by an elderly Christian friend. She had led many to the Lord and watched the changes in their lives. She commented that prior to conversion, people usually simply refer to God as "God." They think of Him as a "Higher Power," or "the Man Upstairs." However, when they receive Him, they suddenly, unconsciously, become aware that He is a person who can be contacted. Then Jesus becomes more than a historic figure in the pages of an antiquated book, and they join with His disciples in calling Him "Lord." In prayer, that becomes "Dear Lord," "loving heavenly Father," or some other expression of love and trust.

As we know from Scripture, what has happened is that, by His grace and mercy, He has actually adopted us as His children. Though we may feel little different (are we always conscious that we are our human father's child?), we

begin to talk to God in a new way and it may be for the
first time. What happens in the new birth is that His Holy
Spirit enters into us, takes our innate capability and desire
for relationship, renews it, and turns it toward God. Then,
just like tiny children reaching out to their parents, we
begin talking to Him, we begin praying.

The Holy Spirit Creates a Family Relationship

When we become part of God's family, we respond in the
same way. We have an assurance that He cares and will
hear us, so we start to direct our worries and our fears, as
well as our joys, toward Him.

Centuries ago, the reformers in Scotland paraphrased 1
John 3 so their people could learn and echo scriptural
truths in praise. Imagine them, meeting in secret, huddled
in their plaids on a misty moor, disenfranchised and pursued by the King's redcoats. What a source of joy and
encouragement to be able to sing:

> Behold, the amazing gift of love
> The Father has bestowed
> On us, the sinful sons of men,
> To call us sons of God.

Though they were nothing in the eyes of men, they
knew that their true significance and their hope depended
upon their relationship with God, restored in Christ. In the
midst of hardship and persecution, they could cry out with
assurance to almighty God because they also knew Him to
be their loving Father.

True prayer, therefore, is based on a genuine relationship to the very person of God Himself through the finished work of the Savior on Calvary's hill. Though that

happened two thousand years ago, the results are applied to His people, in whatever century and wherever they live, by the Holy Spirit, when He wakes us up and gives us eyes to see. Then we cry out to His Father and our Father, to His God and our God.

The Christians in the first century found this to be true when they read the book *Shepherd of Hermas* and began to understand what it means to be the bride of Christ. The Scottish Covenanters, fifteen hundred years later, found the same, and today, the same eternal Spirit is the one who comes into us with the spirit of adoption to lead us out in confident prayer to our Father.

True Prayer — the First Sign of Conversion

The New Testament teaches us through the account of the Apostle Paul's life that one of the first effects of the new birth is the beginning of true prayer. In Acts 9, the first account of Paul's conversion on the road to Damascus, we read that the Lord told Ananias, a local Christian, to go and find Saul of Tarsus. But Saul had been on his way to put to death the believers in that city. Naturally Ananias was worried about how he could be sure that Saul's attitude was totally changed!

But even before he could express his fears, God said just one thing to him: "Behold, he is praying." In other words, "Look, he is praying. Look! Look! He's different now, Ananias. Don't be fearful of this man who has been killing Christians up and down the land. Don't worry about him anymore; why, he is praying! Saul is someone who can be trusted now — the fact that he's a praying man proves it!"

Paul had been a religious man before. He had been a "Pharisee of the Pharisees," a high-ranking religious leader, well educated in all of the official forms of prayer. However, as Jesus says in Matthew 6, that kind of praying does not break through to God. But now for the first time in his life, this Pharisee was really praying! The big difference was that on the Damascus road he had met the risen Jesus.

As Hallesby reminds us, prayer is the risen Jesus coming in with His resurrection power, given free rein in our lives, and then using His authority to enter any situation and change things.[3] That is precisely what He did in Saul of Tarsus' life: prayer was the first sign of the divine presence.

There may be someone reading this who has never really prayed in all his life. You have certainly been a decent person, maybe even a religious person, with a good background like Saul of Tarsus, but you have never really felt that you have made contact with the heavenly Father. Yes, He is infinite, all-knowing, and sovereign, but He is also personal, because He is a father. So you can take courage. There is no need to feel condemned for your failure. Instead you can ask Him to send the risen Christ into your prayerless heart. When He enters as Lord, with the forgiveness won for you on the cross, then you will be able to pray as never before!

Hallowed be Thy name.
(Matthew 6:9)

2

PRAYER AND THE PRAISE OF GOD

The Lord's Prayer has traditionally been thought of as being divided into six petitions or requests. So far we have been studying the first line of the first petition, to identify the one to whom we are making our requests. However, this first petition does not stop with God's nature but goes on to speak of His name — "hallowed be Your name." So we must now spend some time thinking about the importance of God's name in prayer and specifically what it means "to hallow His name."

What's in a Name

How was your name chosen? Did your parents simply like the sound of the name they selected? Maybe you were named for a family member, or even for someone famous at the time of your birth. Not every culture decides on names in this way. Think of the American Indian names that have come down to us in stories of the Old West: Chief Sitting Bull, Singing Grass, Eagle Feather. Such names were selected with a purpose. It was hoped, and indeed believed, that the characteristics expressed by the name would in some way become part of the personality of the growing child.

Similarly, in the Biblical world of thought, a person's name has much more significance than it generally does in modern Europe and America. Rather than just an accidental group of sounds that the parents chose for a child, the name stands for the whole character and, in one sense, represents the reality of that person. A name is expressive of what a person really is and does. Thus, to the Hebrew mind, God's name stood for God himself. Of course, since the names of God given in the Bible are the *revealed* names of God, then in His case alone, His name and His nature are one and the same.

We can see this in phrases such as these from Psalm 5:11 and Psalm 20:1: "Let those also who love Your *name* be joyful in You" (emphasis added); "May the *name* of the God of Jacob defend you" (emphasis added). In other words: Let those who love *You* be joyful in You; and may the *person of God* defend you. Many centuries ago, my ancestors in Scotland took as a family motto the verse from Proverbs, "The name of the Lord is a strong tower; the righteous run to it and are safe" (18:10). An appropriate motto indeed because in those days the Scottish clans were always fighting one another! And of course, what they were desiring was that God Himself would protect them!

So the name stands for God Himself and also for the divine perfections. In Exodus 34:5–7, as God is revealing His Name, He goes on to list His perfections. In other words, this is exactly the same thing as telling His people what He is like. We read that "the LORD descended in the cloud and stood with him [Moses] there, and proclaimed the name of the LORD." And what exactly is that name?

The verse continues, "The LORD passed before him and proclaimed, 'The LORD, the LORD God, merciful and gracious, longsuffering, and abounding in goodness and truth, keeping mercy for thousands, forgiving iniquity and transgression and sin, by no means clearing the guilty.'" Surely, this is the kind of God to whom prayer would be worthwhile!

According to the Old Testament, these divine perfections of God's name offered great encouragement in the lives of His people and were a controlling factor in their praying. There are many different names of God given in the Scriptures, and each one tells us something specific about what God wills for the person who is using this name to call on Him. You may remember some of these names: *Elohim* seems to speak of His divine transcendence, *Yahweh* (or *Jehovah*) of His saviorhood, *El Shaddai* of His massive power, and *Jireh* of His graciousness to provide.

Name Recognition

In my wife's hometown of Cambridge, England, which is full of beautiful, historic architecture, new facilities have been built for the increasing number of students at the University. The country's best architects were sought out, with the goal of producing examples of the best modern design to go along with world-famous buildings, such as King's College and the Wren Library.

But reaction to the results has been very mixed. Many people have been quite unable to see anything attractive in the jutting angles and irregular features of some of the modern structures. Some critics have gone so far as to say that such buildings are nothing more than a "monument to the architect." All that has been achieved, they say, is that the architect has "made a name for himself" that will go down through history—and they do not mean this as a compliment!

Whether or not these critics are saying anything about the original motivation of these designers, such a desire for personal and historical recognition was indeed in the minds of some who were planning a city in the ancient Near East. Apparently soon after the flood, when people were spreading out again over the earth, many realized that power and influence could be had if, instead of wandering as nomads, they built a dazzling city and a tower "whose top is in the heavens" (Genesis 11:4).

Yet God personally came down, the text tells us, and scattered them all over the earth so that their project came to nothing. Furthermore, He deliberately reduced their power by destroying the unity that they had through a common language.

What was it about their plans that drew down such drastic judgment from God? It was this matter of motivation. They desired to make a *name* for themselves. This is the essence of sin, the root of all rebellion against God, and reveals the desire to be "Number One" over against God. He knew that, in the flush of their success, these early people would let their imaginations run wild, throw over all restraint, and forget His righteousness altogether. Power and pride would become their downfall. Are we any different?

Who Comes First?

Now note, in contrast, that the essence of Old Testament piety is defined in Psalm 115:1 where it says, *"Not unto us, O Lord, not unto us, but to Your name give glory"* (emphasis added). The ultimate example of the one who put

God first was Jesus. God's name was the most precious thing to Him as He faced the unspeakable death of the cross and all that would be involved in His being "made . . . sin for us" (2 Corinthians 5:21). When He was about to be separated from the Father on our account, in order to deliver every believer from the pains of hell, He was sustained throughout His incredible suffering for us by thinking of the name of God. Yet, as Jesus was literally facing those pains of hell Himself, He prayed, "Now My soul is troubled, and what shall I say? 'Father, save Me from this hour'? But for this purpose I came to this hour. Father, glorify Your *name*" (John 12:27–28, emphasis added).

The very basis on which Jesus faced the cross for His people, *"Father, hallowed be Your name,"* was no superficial formula, but the sincere response of His whole soul to the glory of God as well as to the needs of His people. This was the attitude that took Him through the Garden of Gethsemane as well as through the infinite sufferings of Calvary.

A remarkable glimpse into the personal relationship between the Father and the Son is in the description in John's gospel of an episode that occurs the week before the Crucifixion. Throughout His life, Jesus resisted any efforts to precipitate events. He would always say, "My hour is not yet come. . . ." In John 12, Jesus finally acknowledges that the time has indeed come, but notice what He actually says: "The hour has come that the Son of Man should be *glorified*" (v. 23, emphasis added). He sums up the underlying purpose of His whole life in just one phrase that is the equivalent of "hallowed be Your name." Surely this emphasizes for us the importance of this part of the Lord's Prayer. If Jesus' supreme purpose was to see glory brought to God, should not ours be the same?

He goes on to describe the necessity and significance of sacrificial death, for Himself and His followers. Suddenly, the shadow of the coming agony of Gethsemane seems to fall across Him, and He cries: "Now My soul is troubled, . . . 'Father, save Me from this hour'" (v. 27). But the very purpose of His coming becomes the source of His strength to endure the cross, for He continues: "Father, glorify Your *name*" (v. 28, emphasis added). And what does the Father say in response? How does He sum up the life of His Son? "I have both *glorified* [My name] and will *glorify* it again [in what You are going to do]" (John 12:28, emphases added).

In Jesus' Name

As the name of the Father was of the utmost concern to the Son, so the name of the Son is of the utmost concern to the Father. This is why we must pray "in Jesus' name."

When a believer faithfully uses the name of Jesus in prayer, the Father can let that prayer walk right through the throne room of heaven and up to His very heart, for He hears the voice of His beloved Son in its tones! When I come in Jesus' name, it is as though Christ takes my hand and we walk up to the Father's throne together. The Father can accept me because I am related to Him through the Son. "He has made us," as it says in Ephesians, "accepted in the Beloved" (1:6).

The basis of this acceptance is, of course, the death of Christ for us. When I come to pray, my prayers come through the blood; my person comes through the blood; my needs come through the blood directly to God, for I am accepted because of the blood shed on my behalf. Pleading the name of the sacrificial Lamb gains me admittance and a hearing.

Building on this truth, the famous reformer of Geneva, John Calvin, states most graphically the meaning of "praying in the name of Jesus." In his commentary on Hebrews 10:19, he writes, "The blood of Christ is always distilling before the presence of the Father."[1]

Now not many of those who read this kind of book will be familiar with backwoods stills or any other kind of still for that matter. The principle, of course, is that as heat is applied, boiling liquid is forced through a series of curling tubes, reducing and concentrating it to a high alcoholic content. Just as the distillation process purifies and brings a liquid down to its basic essence, Calvin says it is as though the blood of Christ is always flowing up in heaven, purifying and concentrating within it the prayers of those He bought with that blood.

Hallowing God's Name through Obedience

The name of God is of central importance, so it is not at all surprising that Jesus makes the first petition of the Lord's Prayer: "Hallowed be Your name."

Hallowed means let His name be *holy*, let it be *sanctified*, let it be *praised*, let it be *prized*. *Hallowed* is the same word in 1 Peter 3:15, "But sanctify [or hallow] the Lord God in your hearts," meaning set Christ apart on a solitary throne, give Him the preeminence.

To make Him preeminent is in fact the essence of true worship and the basis of a meaningful life of real Biblical prayer. Our attitude should be one of bowing down to Him. In other words, prayer cannot be thought of as just talking to God, because it is closely connected with our willingness to obey Him. Prayer is, after all, an expression of faith, and as James reminds us, "faith without works is dead" (James 2:20).

Thus, when we say something like "hallowed be Your name," meaning "sanctify Your name," or "put Yourself on the throne of my heart," it could mean applying the cross to our selfishness and our egocentricity, to our desire always to be first and to get our own way. So if we pray this kind of prayer, we will begin to experience the work of the cross in our life. The cross spells death to our desires to play with sin, and death hurts! Many of us are experiencing pain for this reason in our lives right now.

But that is no reason to be discouraged. The paradox of the Christian life, and particularly of Christian service, is that every time we are willing to allow the discipline of the cross to be applied in our lives then we begin to experience resurrection power. When we are prepared for God to have His way, for Him to be first, or even for another person to be first for the sake of Christ, our pride in our own abilities comes under attack, and we experience a death to self. But, because Jesus defeated the power of death on the cross, the power of His resurrection can follow our crosses, too. It reminds us again of what Hallesby said, "True praying is to ask the risen Christ to come in."[2]

Self-Denial Bears Lasting Fruit

A cousin of mine recently died at ninety-three years of age. She had been in poor health for several years, but her son, who lived with her, was committed to caring for her at home. Whom did he find in the community to help him? The two dear Christian women who ultimately helped him bear the load were both mothers of six or seven children.

We often commented that it was no accident that they should be prepared to do such work. Caring for a large number of children, as those of you who have children can understand, had long ago taught them to give up self-rights under the constant barrage of demands and needs of others! Yet they were not beaten down and angry at having had to work so hard. In fact, the self-denial practiced then bore fruit in a deeply rooted Christian faith and was the source of their willing spirit of service years later.

Insofar as we avoid the discipline of the cross and avoid truly saying, "Hallowed be Thy name" at our own expense, then our Christian walk begins to lose a sense of reality because we are losing touch with the risen Savior. Thus the kind of prayer that sometimes takes us down to the foot of the cross and accepts suffering and self-denial opens the flood of power. We shall gain far more than we lose every time. God is such a generous God. He has designed the rivers of light and life and love to flow down precisely at the place where there is the yielding of self and self rights to "hallow His name."

Hallowing God's Name through Praise

We have already seen that hallowing God's name means putting His will first in the choices of our daily lives. But what does it mean specifically to hallow God's name when we pray? Surely it means to offer Him sincere praise for who He is and what He does.

Recently, one of our children made the honor roll at his school for the first time. That meant that his name was included in the list given to the local paper. It was a new experience to be publicly recognized! Along with the others on the roll, he was "set apart" and received praise for it. Think of praising God in that way, mentally placing His name at the top of the roll of those whom you respect and honor. Is there anyone worthy of more praise?

The Bible is full of practical suggestions as to why and how we may praise God or hallow His name. An entire book of the Old Testament is known in Hebrew as *The Book of Praises* and has more chapters than any other book of the Bible. We call it the *Book of Psalms*. The model prayer begins its first petition with praise: "hallowed [sanctified, uplifted] be Your name." Likewise, praise should be at the very beginning of everything in our praying, the first thought as we get up in the morning and our last when we go to bed at night.

Perhaps you wish to praise God, but you find it hard to know how. John Calvin, can help us here, too. In *The Institutes of the Christian Religion*, Book III, chapter 20, he says that one of the first things we have to remember when we want to praise God is that it is, indeed, often difficult to praise Him. He writes: "We ought to hate our inertia and seek the aid of the Holy Spirit whenever we want to praise God. Our hearts are so cold and we so badly need a burning desire to praise God."[3]

In other words, even if we are true believers and realize something of what God is like, it is not necessarily natural for a great stream of praise and benediction to flow through our innermost beings and loosen our tongues to praise Him. John Calvin's solution is ask the Holy Spirit at the beginning of prayer to open us up and enable us to praise the Lord with His own help.

Scripture-Based Praise

How will the Holy Spirit help us do this? He may bring to mind experiences of God's dealing with us which show us the wonders of His divine character. But we will also do well to base our praises on the Spirit-inspired scriptural revelation of His nature, His mighty deeds, and His grace.

For instance you could take a passage like Philippians 2:5–11 that speaks first of all of the humiliation and the exaltation of Christ, of how He humbled himself to death on our behalf and how God has highly exalted Him and given Him a name that is above every name. But then look at the very next phrase. The purpose of His exaltation is, "that at the name of Jesus every knee should bow . . . and . . . every tongue should confess that Jesus Christ is Lord.".

Right there, we have a perfect example of how a description of the character and acts of God should draw a response of praise. And notice how the heart of this verse follows exactly our Lord's teaching to hallow the divine name. Praise God for everything about Jesus that we read here.

Everyone is familiar with the story of the old farmer who would tumble into bed after an exhausting day's work, glance up at the cross-stitched version of the Lord's Prayer on the wall, and mumble, "Them's my sentiments exactly, Lord"! Now we are not suggesting something quite as brief as that! But he was on the right track in that he was echoing the revealed words of Scripture.

The idea is to take a passage, read through it slowly, and then use those words and phrases to tell the Lord of our love and adoration. We can say, "Amen" to what we read, repeat it in our own words, or go further and use the Bible as a springboard for our own expressions of praise.

Take Genesis 1:1, for example. "In the beginning God created the heavens and the earth." Once there was nothing in existence at all except God — and then He created everything. Praise Him for it. Praise Him for the creation that you see around you, or simply praise Him for the power and imagination He has displayed in His creative acts. Praise Him that you have eyes to see, and that He has revealed Himself to you so that you now know that He is the Creator.

Or perhaps you could select a particular psalm. Psalm 103 is a wonderful aid to praise because it does not include even one request! It has often been called "the psalm of unmingled praise." It begins, "Bless the Lord, O my soul, and forget not all His benefits." Read slowly through the Psalm: notice how He heals, how He forgives our iniquities, how He removes them as far as the east is from the west, how He renews our youth, how He fills our mouth with good things. As you go, add your own praises to those of King David.

Revelation 5 is another passage you could use. Join with the chorus of the angels and the saints. Maybe even imagine yourself joining with loved ones who have preceded you to glory! What are they doing, hour by hour, face to face with the living God? John tells us he heard them crying, "Worthy is the Lamb who was slain to receive power and riches and wisdom, and strength and honor and glory and blessing!" (Revelation 5:12).

In your time of prayer, you can echo the singing in heaven and praise, with them, the Lamb that was slain. You may even want to sing out loud some of the paraphrases of the psalms which are included in the hymnbook, or use other hymns that express praise.

Sincerity in Praise

The third thing we need for true praise is to give God our whole heart. Psalm 9 begins, "I will praise You, O LORD, with my whole heart." Put another way, that means to give God our full attention.

You know how worrisome it is if you are trying to talk to a person who is looking away from you, perhaps talking to someone else or even turning up their television a little bit louder! You have something that you thought was worth hearing, but they ignore you. We know how that feels because we have all done it and have had it done to us. Do you realize that God knows, and really cares, whether He has our attention or not, or whether our eyes are focused on Him? And so He will help us here. When we come to praise God at the beginning of our prayers, we are to ask Him to help us give Him our full attention.

There was a remarkable man, known as Brother Lawrence, who lived in the seventeenth century. He was a cook in a monastery kitchen not far from Paris, yet out of his humble and rather insignificant position in that monastery, he wrote a book that has been a blessing to many entitled *The Practice of the Presence of God.*[4]

With all the multitude of things that he had to do in the monastery kitchen — washing dishes, cooking huge pans of eggs, or scrubbing the floors — he nevertheless learned how to praise God continually, in the midst of all the noisy hustle and bustle. He used to take a mental "time-out" and briefly direct his attention to God, offer Him a few words of praise and adoration, and then continue with his duties. His life became such a channel of praise to God that it affected his whole personality. He became such a blessing to those around him that many people, even bishops and leaders of state, began to come from all over Europe to seek his advice.

He had never left his kitchen to learn this secret of experiencing God's presence, and he stayed there throughout his life. He had simply begun praising God where he was and had learned the secret of giving his full attention to God. That is what made his prayers count. That one thing transformed his life and gave him a tremendous ministry right where he was, in a lowly, nonprestigious, menial job.

We, too, can praise God wherever we are, in the most improbable of situations. Even if you have to be in the kitchen a great deal, cheer up! All God asks for is your whole heart, and you can learn to give Him that in the kitchen, the school, the shop, the office, or the marketplace.

Praising God Can Bring Personal Blessing

We praise God, or hallow His name, simply because He deserves it. As the book of Revelation says: "Worthy is the Lamb to receive . . . honor and glory and blessing" (5:12). And yet, it is surely not wrong to add that people who praise God with their whole hearts, receive great personal benefit. What are some of the benefits that come to us when we praise the Lord?

Praising God with our whole being is part of the program that God uses to restore the balance between the different parts of our personality, a balance that was disturbed at the Fall and has caused us all kinds of problems ever since. Thus prayer and praise become part of our sanctification, restoring His image in us and bringing out the best in us.

A great nineteenth-century American Southern Presbyterian theologian, Dr. B. M. Palmer of New Orleans, speaks eloquently in his *Theology of Prayer* of how praise brings blessing into our broken lives.[5] As we direct our attention to the living God and try to praise Him as He deserves, it forces us to use all our mental and emotional faculties in the ways for which they were originally designed.

Delighted and amazed at the health-giving power of prayer, Dr. Palmer lists the effects on each part of our personality as we focus away from ourselves toward God and His person and will as revealed in Scripture.

For example, he shows how beginning to grasp the nature of God as seen in the Scriptures and then seeing how we are related to Him can become the basis of a correct understanding of reality in general. He contends that our ability to make value judgments comes under scrutiny as we bring our circumstances before God and have to decide if a particular request is really legitimate and necessary. Furthermore, our consciences receive the best opportunity to develop when we go to the Lord in prayer to seek a course of action that would be in line with God's law.

Our emotions and will are also influenced by hallowing God's name. Just to see God, Dr. Palmer continues, "in the loveliness of His being" and to make Him our "supreme object of worship and desire," stirs up our emotions and puts them to their best use. And when our will, so indispensable in "translating our thoughts and purposes into the acts which make up the history of human life," is brought to the foot of the cross, permanent changes can occur in our lives.

In other words, every part of our personality will be affected, and "render its quota of service when man bows in worship before that God, whose dim, dark shadow he himself is."

A modern writer, Dr. Paul Billheimer, also points to the same kind of thing in more contemporary terminology. He demonstrates the psychological value of praise when he writes:

> A major reason for offering praise early in prayer is the fact that, in its very nature, praise is unselfish. . . . Here is one of the greatest values of praise: it decentralizes self. The worship and praise of God demands a shift of center from self to God. One cannot praise God without relinquishing occupation with self. Praise produces forgetfulness of self—and forgetfulness of self is health.[6]

Praise Routs the Enemy

Praising God with the whole heart, on the basis of the revealed Word, not only brings spiritual and emotional blessings, but sometimes the results are truly amazing and completely change material circumstances. In 2 Chronicles 20, we are shown how the praise of the glorious, triumphant God actually expels the power of evil from our midst.

In the time of good King Jehoshaphat, a large number of enemies had poured in against Judea. Although God's people were outnumbered, they were still trusting Him and had decided to go out and fight for all they were worth. Jehoshaphat mobilized the army, but he also asked the people of Israel to fast and pray before they took action.

After he assembled the people for battle, he did an interesting thing, a very odd thing that we would never do in a modern warfare. He ordered the women and children to come out in front of the army made up of their husbands and fathers. Next he had the priest and the choir from the temple come out as well, to the very front ranks of the soldiers drawn up in battle formation.

Then, the record says, they began to praise the "beauty of holiness," and an extraordinary thing happened. As they began to sing and to praise this glorious God, His power fell and the soldiers in the enemy army began to destroy one another. The plan of Satan had been to wipe out Israel and thus prevent the coming of a Messiah who could bring salvation to the whole world. But he was foiled by praises sung by tiny children! His troops were routed by killing one another! When God's people came to the scene, all that was left were heaps of dead bodies, laden with so much spoil that it took three whole days to carry it all away!

You say, "Why did that happen?" How, indeed, could a thing like that happen? I believe the key is given in Psalm 22:3 which says, "But You are holy, who inhabit the praises of Israel." In other words, when God's people praise Him there is a sense in which a special presence falls from heaven with power to expel evil. It is said that the Devil hates to hear singing and that he cannot sing a single note. As God's people sing and praise Him and His Son in the Holy Spirit, His presence can fall, as it did into the enemy camp. In our own battles, also, Satan can be expelled by singing.

Praise Takes Us Out of Ourselves

Praise is not a cheap psychological technique to enable you to get rid of something that is bothering you. No! We praise God because of who He is. He is "our chief end," as the Westminster Catechism tells us. However, it is in fact also true that as we praise Him a certain atmosphere is established.

Friends of ours had a son and daughter who were always at each other's throats, fussing and fighting. In particular, the older brother was always ridiculing his sister. Desperate to stop the unpleasantness, the parents suggested that instead of criticizing her, he should find something good to say about her. For every unkind attack, he had to come up with two compliments! He had to look for something good in her.

At first it was like squeezing water from a stone, as the boy scratched his head, completely unable to acknowledge that there was any good in his little sister. Over the months, however, his attitude began to change, and now, several years later, the feelings between them and the mood in the home have vastly improved.

The great theologian and revivalist of New England, Jonathan Edwards, said in his beautiful book, *Charity and Its Fruits*, that when there is much praise in our home, the atmosphere of heaven inevitably comes down. The peace and joy present where the One whom we praise is enthroned flows down to earth when we focus on Him and His goodness in all circumstances. But when there is much complaining in a home, then we lose any trace of a heavenly atmosphere, so that our home becomes more like hell![7]

Praise takes us outside ourselves, above all our petty worries, and catches us up in something wonderful and ennobling. It catches us up into the very purposes and the person of God. Somehow, the beauty of the Lord our God begins to descend upon His people. The result is that the works of their hands and the petitions of their hearts and lips begin to be established and to come to pass. Then, indeed, His name begins to be glorified.

This is our God: so rich in grace, delighting in mercy, personal, infinite, triune, who loves us and saves us in Jesus. He deserves the praises of our hearts.

Jesus says the basis for life as well as the basis for the first thing we ask in daily prayer is "Our Father in heaven, hallowed be Your name." The writers of the Westminster Catechism were absolutely right when they began: "The chief end of man, is to glorify God, and enjoy Him forever." As we, too, begin to understand and live on this basis, then we will realize that we do indeed have access to the "key of life."

Thy kingdom come.
Thy will be done
in earth, as it is in heaven.
(Matthew 6:10)

3

PRAYER AND THE PURPOSES OF GOD

I magine how absurd it would be if the newly elected President stood up on Inauguration Day and in his address to the Nation offered no outline of the goals of the government, and no plan for executing the platform on which he had been elected! It would be a contradiction in terms for a leader to have no plans upon which to act! Leadership assumes the power to make policy and the power to carry it out.

A Sovereign God

We began our study of prayer by seeing that the character of the infinite, personal God is the foundation of all prayer, which is why the first petition of the Lord's Prayer begins: "Our Father, in heaven." But the Bible has given us other information about God that will help us start in the right place and then continue in the right way with our own requests. In the first place, He is sovereign.

Now the word *sovereign* is generally used in the context of government, meaning "one that exercises supreme authority." It is not a word that we use much in the United States, as it is synonymous with *king*, and we have replaced the rule of one man with a government made up of three branches designed to balance the power both to make policy and carry it out. Most modern states are similar. The ruling party is the one with the power to implement the agenda.

Ephesians 1:11 describes God as one, "who works all things according to the counsel of His will." We have here a picture of a sovereign God with a total plan for all history. We discover that our Father, the one whom we have already seen to be the infinite, personal, trinitarian God, is seated on His throne of power and is working out everything in accordance with His perfect plan. He is not an impassive observer over His kingdom but is actively involved in our very existence, always working on something.

No one builds a house or bridge without some kind of plan or blueprint in their mind or on paper. They have not only a design, but also a schedule for implementing that design. So, in the same way, God has a "blueprint," — the counsel of His will — that He is carrying out to the last detail, day by day, year by year, age to age.

The Power of One Man's Prayer

But there is another completely different kind of picture that illustrates the second important truth about prayer: it changes *history*. God works out His will here on the earth He has created, in space and time. This is not some vague, spiritual, intangible reality!

Have you ever read in the history books of a man named, Jabez? Probably not! Yet he is given specific mention in Jewish history, albeit nearly hidden in the long genealogies of 1 Chronicles (see chapter 4:9–10).

In these ancient historical chronicles, families are usually listed, generation after generation, only pausing to draw attention to some great and famous figure who made a significant contribution to history. But 1 Chronicles 4:9–10 records details of the life of a man who is not mentioned anywhere else at all. Evidently his praying and the answer he received were truly remarkable. His prayer was just as significant in the annals of eternity as the political and military and religious leadership usually given special recognition. In one paragraph, his life is summed up:

> Now Jabez was more honorable than his brothers, and his mother called his name Jabez, saying, "Because I bore him in pain." [In other words, his name in Hebrew means literally: "He will cause pain."] And Jabez called on the God of Israel, saying, "Oh that You would bless me indeed and enlarge my territory, that Your hand would be with me, and that You would keep me from evil, that I may not cause pain!" And God granted him what he requested.

Jabez asked God for specific, personal blessings. First of all, he asked for help in business, and then he requested help in his behavior toward others, because he was obviously concerned that his name might reflect his personality and he did not want to be someone who caused pain all his life. His prayer was not particularly elaborate, nor was it couched in flowery, religious language. He simply expressed his basic desires and life-goals to the Father.

Notice that there is no reason to believe that God answered only part of his prayer. We are specifically told that God did grant it. Sometimes we tend to think that it is easier for God to solve spiritual or psychological problems

and that maybe we should not ask Him for material blessings. In fact, to ask God to change a personality — as Jabez
did — is far from easy and may have taken many years!

There is no area we should not bring before Him in
prayer; that is what Jabez' experience assures us. After all,
God created every part of reality and interacts with it all.

At all events, when Jabez prayed, the sovereign God
on His throne was so honored by the fact that he looked to
Him, that He reached down and changed things. Not only
did He grant Jabez' requests, He made him an honored
saint for all eternity. He is included in Jewish history because his prayer is what brought down the power of God
into every area of his life and affected the little corner of
history around him.

So we have two pictures to hold in our minds: a sovereign God and an ordinary man with genuine power because he looked to that God in prayer.

God Has a Plan

Because God is a person we are not only able to communicate with Him also we can assume He will act with *purpose.* One of the characteristics of being a person is the
ability to think ahead and make plans for the future. There
is a need to attempt to exert some control over the future.

Of course, that is all part of our being made in the
image of God. Thus as B. B. Warfield of Princeton said,
once given the reality of an all-powerful, personal God,
the next thing that inevitably follows is an all-encompassing plan.[1] Without one, there would be total disorder and
chaos. God's actions, His words, and everything about
Him are all controlled by a supreme purpose. He knows

the beginning from the end and has known it all from eternity.

Because He is perfect, He makes no mistakes or false starts. Nothing happens at random with God. There is no such thing as chance or luck or even fate, because He has planned it all in love. The God who is in control has a personal interest in what is happening as He fulfills His purpose.

History shows us that when God's person is denied, purpose soon drops out of life. Indeed, Burckhardt, in his famous *Civilization of the Renaissance in Italy,* brilliantly discussed the results of the fifteenth- and sixteenth-century European intellectual replacement of God-centered Christianity by a renewed form of classical man-centered paganism.

He devoted an entire chapter to demonstrating how denying the personal God of Scripture, who controlled the world by His providence, was followed by the reintroduction of ancient ideas of fate, chance, fortune, and superstition.[2] But with the coming of the sixteenth-century Protestant Reformation and the Roman Catholic Counter-Reformation, belief in God was restored to the center of European life and, with it, a sense of purpose and meaning.

A Biblical worldview gives mankind the assurance that the world is not locked into a rigid, impersonal, or possibly even cruel fatalism. In fact we are invited to learn about and participate in God's purposes. The very next stage of the Lord's Prayer deals with the plan or purpose of God: "Your kingdom come, Your will be done on earth as it is in heaven." This is where the first and second pictures come together: the place where the sovereign God and someone as insignificant as you or I can meet.

His Plan Defined

Jesus gives some practical direction in the second and third petitions of the Lord's Prayer, teaching us to pray that the *plan* of God will be accomplished in the world thereby glorifying the name of the Father. God's plan is to be worked out in the establishing of His *kingdom*, His rule here on earth, but the world at present is under the power of sin and Satan. This is where our second picture offers encouragement.

Although Jesus assures us in John 16:33 that He has overcome the world, the prayers of ordinary people like Jabez, and you and me, have a real place. They are a primary means of bringing His victory to bear, in matters that affect us individually, as well as throughout the whole range of national and international affairs. Prayer releases blessing, changes lives, builds up churches, assaults the devil, and brings revival to communities, even to nations. The cries of insignificant members of society really can have a transforming effect on that society.

The story of Jabez is an example of how one man's prayer affected his own immediate sphere of influence. But there have been times in history, probably far more often than we will ever know, when prayer has been the deciding factor in the outcome of crises which threatened a nation.

One such instance was during the time of Queen Elizabeth I of England. The Spanish were planning to invade the country and, among other things, enforce Roman Catholicism on the newly reformed Protestant Church. As the Spanish admirals gathered hundreds of ships in preparation, congregations all over England went to their knees in urgent prayer.

The *Armada* set out in the spring of 1588, but never landed in England. After several skirmishes in the English Channel, terrific storms came up which scattered the Spanish fleet, driving many of the ships so far off course that they returned home by sailing around the north of Scotland!

There is a sense in which the world exists for the sake of the church, to provide a bride for the Son of God. Thus when Jesus teaches us to pray "Thy kingdom come," He is concerned first and foremost with the well-being of His church. On the basis of this line in the Lord's Prayer, those early Protestants felt that they could beseech God to protect the whole country from the threatened invasion. And the country benefited from the presence of a praying church.

Prayer is also necessary to keep the church herself strong and pure, so that the gospel will be effectively preached and bring many to salvation. And prayer will ensure that the church retains the true qualities of salt, affecting society as a whole by preserving it from decay. In other words, it is no accident that where there is a strong church, violent crime is seldom a problem. For example, observers have noted a strong similarity between two otherwise dramatically different islands: the Roman Catholic island of Malta, in the Mediterranean, and the strongly Calvinist Isle of Lewis, off the northwest coast of Scotland.

For years and years, no murders were committed on these islands. In fact, when one occurred in Malta in early 1960, the whole population was in shock, so unaccustomed were they to such behavior in a country where nearly everyone was a faithful churchgoer, well aware of the ten commandments. Similar shock waves swept over Lewis in the early 1970s when an elderly lady was killed by an escapee from a psychiatric hospital who entered her unlocked home.

The *Westminster Larger Catechism* reminds us that when we pray for the world, God's intervention in the general affairs of men will always be contingent upon His plan for the church. But it is also true that a strong church will bring blessing to society at large, as the dominion of Satan is rolled back.

Finally, in this petition, we see that the ultimate goal of our prayers and the supreme need of all creation is for Christ's return. Then the kingdom will come in its entirety, with the ultimate defeat of Satan at the end of time. However, until then, the fact that we are to pray for the earth at all is an indication that God takes this material existence seriously. God's purposes include this sinful, rebellious planet here and now. This is where He wants His name to be glorified.

Two Complementary Truths

But notice something very remarkable: Jesus is telling us that our prayers are part of the outworking of those purposes! We are given a mandate to become involved in His divine plan through our human praying. He invites us to approach Him with earthly needs, just like Jabez or those who prayed against the Spanish *Armada*. Our prayer can be effective in seeing that the divine "will is done."

If this were not so, God would simply tell us that His kingdom will come, that we are not to worry. All that we would have to do would be simply to obey His revealed will and not pray for it! But in some extraordinary way, the unchanging, sovereign God, with an eternally defined purpose for His creatures, invites our input into the making of history.

As we think about praying for the plan of God to come to pass in our lives and in the whole world, we can keep the right perspective if we hold together in our minds these two tremendous, Biblical truths. The first is that God has an all-encompassing plan and is utterly sovereign over all. The other is that human prayer really is effective in the supernatural realm.

Whenever these truths are held together, a certain chemistry takes place. Something wonderful happens in those who believe them, hold them together, and practice them. It has remarkable effects both in their prayer life and in their public service.

The Protestant Reformers Changed History

The belief in the sovereignty of God and in the effectiveness of human prayer characterized the lives of the Protestant Reformers who changed not only the face of Europe, but also affected the American Colonies. In fact, we are still basking in the liberty and the prosperity of this chemistry that occurred when these two mighty truths were somehow rediscovered and brought together in the great revival of the sixteenth century.

Like the apostles before them, they literally "turned the world upside down," because they believed that they could make contact with the sovereign ruler of the universe. They had rediscovered the personal nature of God and that they could be united to Him through Christ. Thus they had the confidence that they could bring His power to bear in their own lives and surroundings.

The famous nineteenth-century British essayist, Thomas Carlyle, stated eloquently how many of our most cherished civil rights and free institutions come directly from the sixteenth-century European Reformation and its offspring, the seventeenth-century British Puritan movement.

In a well-known essay, he listed such civil liberties as free parliaments (or congresses), successful replacements of tyrannical governments (as in 1688 in England), and freedom from illegal imprisonment, as guaranteed by the *Habeas Corpus* Act.

These are his words: "The Puritanism of Scotland became that of England, of New England. A tumult in the High Church of Edinburgh spread into a universal battle and struggle over all these realms;—there came out, after fifty-years struggling, what we call the 'Glorious Revolution,' a *Habeas Corpus* Act, Free Parliaments, and much else!"[3]

God Has Planned To Use Our Prayers

Following the example of the Reformers we also must put these two mighty truths together. Only then will we be ready to understand what it means to pray for God's will to be done and for His kingdom to come. The sovereign God on His throne, who has planned all things from the beginning to the end, has arranged His plan in such a way that the prayers of the saints are one of the major means He uses to accomplish His final goal. Instead of the sovereignty of God clashing with the prayers of the believer, the two actually presuppose one another and fulfill and undergird one another.

God made His world and ordered His plan in such a way that when we become burdened and concerned over some situation, He uses it for good, even to further His purposes. In fact, He lays the burden on us. For example we find ourselves under pressure, in a predicament that we cannot resolve, and so we begin to pray.

The fact that God sometimes will cause us to pray by anonymously bringing unusual pressures to bear upon us is like the experience of two C. S. Lewis *Chronicles of Narnia* characters, Shasta and Aravis.

In the delightful story, *The Horse and His Boy*, the hero and heroine – the slave boy, Shasta, and the runaway aristocratic girl, Aravis – are chased or attacked by lions at different points in their dangerous journey. In one instance, they even meet a rather strange, but apparently ordinary house cat. These animals keep them from going in the direction they want to go and force them to take an alternate route. How terrible to be set upon by dangerous animals when they were already under the stress of a life-threatening journey!

But at the end of the story, they are amazed and greatly comforted to discover that all the different hostile lions and the strange house cat whom they happened to meet were actually one and the same person: Aslan, the supernatural lion, whom Lewis uses to represent Christ, "the conquering lion of the tribe of Judah."[4]

Had these lions (and the pussy cat) not scared them into taking a different direction, they would have been captured by the enemy and immediately put to death or reduced to slavery. The strange pressure of these frightening attacks were in fact the divine blessing which forced them to travel in a safe pathway.

One day we too will discover that many of the prayers we were forced to pray by our very fears and pains were actually the shadow of the divine blessing to keep us and others from untold tragedy as we were secretly pressed into an unseen Shepherd's fold!

It may be something that affects us personally or a need brought to our attention on the other side of the world. We may be forced to our knees in desperation by an emergency, or we may daily and regularly bring certain requests to the King. Whatever it is that prompts us to come to Him, the fact is that God Himself has ordained that these prayers of His people begin to release predestined blessings which would not have flowed down at all had the prayers not occurred.

Catch the Vision!

Whatever we do, wherever we are, all through life, God has His plan for our daily work, for soul winning, and for preaching. One of the ways He carries out His plan is to activate our personality so that we will pray and then take intelligent action, preach, witness, and serve. In all of it, His plan comes more and more to fruition. His goal begins to be reached through both the prayers and the actions of His people. It is because God planned it to be this way that these two truths—God has a sovereign plan, and a believer has genuine power in prayer to effect the supernatural—are not in fact contradictory, but come together in wonderful harmony.

People who catch the vision of this glorious sovereign God, who has destined the prayers of His people to be a means of executing His unspeakably wonderful decrees, have a way of transforming the world. They have the assurance that the power of God Himself can be brought to bear. Again, Hallesby's description holds good: prayer brings in the presence of the living Christ.[5]

We can see, therefore, how our prayers can bring about the purposes of God and why we should be faithful to Jesus' teaching to pray, "Thy kingdom come." But He gives us further instruction.

Since the first petition of the Lord's Prayer has taught us to put Him first, it should not come as a surprise that, however personally costly it may be, we must echo the third petition. Here Jesus teaches us to say, "Your will be done," when we are seeking God's intervention to transform the world. Our prayers are to be governed by His will, in order that His name — and not ours — will be glorified.

However, the next phrase, "on earth, as it is in heaven," offers enormous encouragement to pray for His intervention when we see that the mandate He has given His people in prayer is no less than to bring His plan to pass. We obviously know very little about heaven from Scripture. But one thing is sure, the atmosphere of praise and worship will surely issue in complete and joyful submission, the kind that would prove that our expressions of praise are really sincere! Yet this is the way things should be here, now. Jesus tells us that the Father desires to have mankind living and acting in obedience with His divine will. So we can never be wrong to pray for that!

The Will of God, Known and Unknown

What is God's will? Traditional theology has thought of the will of God in two different, though related, senses.

First, there is the teaching in the Bible that can be summarized under the title, "the *secret* will of God," also known as His "decretive will." This is the rule which governs His own actions in creation (see Revelation 4:11), in providence (see Daniel 4:35), and in grace (see Romans

9:15). Secondly, we are told of His "*revealed* will," or His "preceptive will." They are not, of course, two different wills, but two aspects of the same divine will.

A. W. Pink explains it this way:

> The will of God, then, is a phrase that, taken by itself, may express *either* what God has *purposed* to do or what He has *commanded* to be done by us. With regard to the will of God in the first sense, it always is, always has been, and ever shall be done upon earth as it is in heaven, for neither human policy nor infernal power can prevent it.

> The text now before us, [i.e. the Lord's Prayer] contains a prayer that we might be brought into complete accord with God's *revealed will.* God's *revealed or preceptive will* is the rule for our actions, God having made known in the Scriptures that which is pleasing in His sight.

> The *secret or decretive will* of God is always done equally on earth as in heaven, for none can thwart or even hinder it. It is equally evident that God's revealed will is violated every time one of His precepts is disobeyed.

> This distinction was clearly drawn when Moses said to Israel, "The *secret* things belong to the Lord our God, but those things which are *revealed* belong to us and to our children forever, that we may do all the words of this Law" (Deuteronomy 29:29).[6] (Emphasis added)

Undoubtedly, therefore, what Christ is teaching us to pray for in the Lord's Prayer has reference to the *revealed will.* We are to pray for those things that are in accordance with Scripture, that are right and proper and will honor His name.

Now a child will often disregard this requirement and make all kinds of fantastic requests. When one of our children was about three-years-old, several friends of ours were at the house for a prayer meeting. Not wishing to be left out, the little fellow prayed earnestly that God would give people all over the world new slides to play on!

Needless to say, one little boy in the community did soon get one. However, as he has grown older, he has had to learn, like all of us, that a generous heart or overwhelming desire for change is not enough when we are deciding what to pray for. We are to be controlled by what we know of the revealed will. We are to pray every day that those things which His Word requires should be done here on earth.

A Hidden Harmony

Although the main emphasis in our prayers must be on the clearly revealed will of God in Scripture, this does not mean that His secret will has no connection with our praying. On the contrary, when we pray on the basis of the revealed will, we are lining ourselves up with the person of God and thus with the secret purposes of God. His secret purposes are carried out through the praying of His saints on the basis of His revealed will in Scripture.

That is not to say that we understand how He is carrying out those purposes. We are not let into the secret of why He is letting strange things happen or why He delays answers to prayer. We may only be able to hazard a guess at the inner workings of God's plan, but we can know that as we pray, "Thy will be done" on the basis of His written Word, our prayers are being caught up in the eternal purposes of God.

There, in the "grinding of the wheels of providence," they are somehow being used to activate the eternal decrees of God in space-time history. That is why tremendous things occur when believers pray "Your will be done." The secret is to take God's promises and desires, as expressed in Scripture, and make them the basis of intercession.

Friends of ours have laughed at how God once answered prayers far beyond what any of us were asking. We were planning to move the whole family, plus two friends, to Scotland for an eight-month sabbatical. We were due to leave in late December, but by mid-November we still had not found anywhere to stay.

We began to wonder if we had misread the Lord's leading and asked our friends to join us in praying that God would confirm that it was His will to go by providing suitable accommodation. We prayed the promise given in Jeremiah 33:3, "Call to Me, and I will answer you, and show you great and mighty things, which you do not know."

Two weeks before we were to leave, we received word that we could stay as long as we needed at a residential research center, though we would be rather cramped. The immediate burden was lifted, and so we set off. But within a month of our arrival, something amazing happened.

A beautiful old house, which had formerly been used as a children's home, was being converted into a different kind of facility, and someone was needed to live there, act as a caretaker, identify the areas in need of repair, and let in the workmen. Not merely was there room for all of us—nine altogether—but there were thirteen bedrooms and six bathrooms! And it was in the most beautiful location, with a huge yard for our boys to play in. These were certainly "great and mighty things, which [we did] not know"!

We had had no choice but to cast ourselves on the will of God. At the time, we wondered what would happen. But He met our needs so perfectly and generously that we discovered firsthand how, in His providence, He can bring together many diverse factors to provide us with the very best.

God's Plan Does Not Rule Out Our Prayer

We have already looked at Ephesians 1:11, when we were considering the fact that an infinite personal God has a sovereign plan, worked out "according to the counsel of His will." This verse actually speaks of all His acts in Christ toward us as being "predestined according to [His] purpose."

The very word *predestination* often raises "red flags"! But we have already begun to find a way to tackle this controversial question. The heart of the problem is that people are so often scared by the thought that God has a fixed plan and that He knows and is in control of everything ahead of time. It seems threatening precisely because it points us to the secret will of God, which is beyond our reach.

However, when we begin to grasp the truth that our prayers can be used as part of the outworking of God's secret will, then we discover that prayer is not at all rendered unnecessary or futile because of the existence of the predestined plan or will of God. Rather, it is the means of actually carrying out that plan.

When we pray, "Your will be done," we are not trying to twist God's arm and say, "Lord, I know that You don't want to do this. But if I bother You long enough, You might change Your mind and do it"! We are not acting like children, pestering reluctant parents, hoping to wear them out till they give in!

On the contrary, when we are stuck in some hard situation and are begging God for His revealed will to be brought to pass, we are actually praying that way because God has put us in the position where we will feel the need to pray! Our praying is, in fact, a preparation for the release of the blessings of God.

Dr. B. M. Palmer gave his congregation some original insight into this mystery when he offered them a helpful look behind the scenes.

> The scriptural principle is not that favors are, by our importunity, wrung from the reluctance of the Divine Being, but that they antedate the prayer in the determinations of His sovereign and gracious will; and the true spirit of prayer, which He also imparts, is the sign and pledge of the gift to be conveyed.

> Prayer, then, as already stated, is not the cause which procures through its own efficiency, but merely the antecedent condition upon which a predetermined benefit is suspended. The purpose to give is, on Jehovah's part, sovereign and free; it is the spontaneous movement of His own gracious and loving will. Yet, in the exercise of the same sovereignty and goodness, He interposes the prayer of the creature as the channel through which His favor shall descend.[7]

Prayer Releases Blessings Already in Store

Because God has purposed in advance to bless us, the result of our prayer is often far greater than we could imagine. As we begin to pray in accordance with the promises of His Word, asking that His will be done in order that His name might be hallowed and glorified, it releases those blessings which He has in store for us. He has deliberately put us into the position where we feel the necessity to pray just so we may learn what He can do and how much He loves us.

Dr. Palmer offers an illustration from Ezekiel 36:37.

God announces to the prophet weeping by the banks of the river Chebar, and through him, to captive Israel, his fixed purpose to restore them to the land of their fathers. In glowing terms, their future prosperity and joy are depicted, with all the privileges which should follow upon a sanctified use of their present sorrows. Yet it is added with solemn emphasis, "I will also let the house of Israel inquire of me to do this for them." How clear the matter stands! Jehovah, in the good pleasure of his will, has firmly resolved to bring back his captive people to the land which was theirs by inheritance from Abraham. It is announced as certain, without qualification or contingency. Yet this revealed purpose will work itself out through the prayer of Israel, which is announced with the same positiveness, as a means to the end, and prescribed as the condition upon which the promised restoration shall be accomplished.[8]

Arguing with God

Successful prayer is ultimately in harmony with the will of God, yet at the same time, there are several instances in the Bible where the saints do seem to argue against a clear decision that the Lord has already made, begging Him to change His mind. That is something that you and I have probably wanted to do many times but have feared that it would be a violation of the instructions to pray, "Your will be done."

And yet if God does seem to respond to such arguing by the great fathers of the faith, maybe we can learn from them how to express our disagreement with what we fear is the final answer to our prayers.

Their experiences offer us clues to know when and how to question God. Notice that these instances in Scripture occur especially where judgment is involved. Abraham, for instance, pleaded against the Lord's clearly announced decision to destroy Sodom and Gomorrah. He asked God to have mercy upon the wicked city if even ten righteous persons could be found within its walls. He took as his premise: "Shall not the Judge of all the earth do right?" (Genesis 18:25). And, indeed, God agreed to do so, although in the end, ten could not be found.

When Jacob was at the brook Jabbok with all of his family and cattle, helpless against the oncoming army of his offended brother, Esau, he spent all night pleading against the military judgment which he knew he deserved at the hand of his cheated brother.

Genesis 32 tells us how he argued with God to avert the impending ruin of his family and wealth, on the basis that they were all blessings to him from the God of mercy and truth (verse 10), and that their destruction (deserved, in a sense, as it was) would be a destruction of the very covenant mercies of the Lord Himself.

In later generations, Moses argued against the Lord's decision to blot out the rebellious children of Israel in the wilderness, declaring that he would rather be destroyed himself if God would not blot out their sins (Exodus 32:32). He more than once reminded the Lord that the destruction of the Hebrews in the wilderness would reflect poorly on the name of the Lord in the ears of the Egyptians.

Finally, in Romans 9:3–4, the Apostle Paul seems to be arguing along these very lines. So much does he long for their salvation, he declares that he could wish himself "accursed from Christ for [his] brethren . . . according to the flesh, . . . [the] Israelites."

One theme underlies all this argumentation against the will of God: the saints refuse to accept as final God's initial signs of anger against His people. In their prayer, they plead for mercy on the basis of *God's own character and His own glory*. So, in pleading against God's immediate decision of judgment, they are arguing on the basis of His eternal character and out of a concern for His greater glory before men.

Thus they are submitted to the fact that He is sovereign, and they want whatever will show Him to be worthy of honor. They are not really asking Him ultimately to go against His own holy character. They honor Him too much for that. Rather, they are pleading for undeserved mercy in accordance with His nature and glory. And our God loves to be talked to on that basis!

This is surely reason enough to agonize and plead for our Western secularist society today, rather than writing it off for its apostasy. We do not need to abandon hope of seeing the Father's will done on earth as in heaven, however deserved or imminent His judgment.

What Prayer Can Do

Willie Black, a former classmate of ours, had a successful pastorate in a small country church in the far north of Scotland. Week by week, for nearly ten years, he faithfully expounded the books of the Bible, chapter by chapter. He grew to love the congregation and saw fruit from the Word sown in their lives.

Wishing to encourage them to take overseas missions seriously, he regularly invited missionary personnel to his church. On one occasion, after introducing a visitor from the Overseas Missionary Fellowship, he sat back to listen to the report on work in the Far East and Korea in particular.

Suddenly he felt as though he had been hit literally by something physical. He sat through the sermon with a sense of being weighted down and could hardly rise at the end of the service to give the closing remarks and benediction. But the feeling gradually left him as the day wore on, and being a practical, down-to-earth Scot, he assumed that by the next day, everything would be back to normal!

Sure enough, when morning came, there was only a trace of the heavy burden. Nevertheless, he was concerned to be alert to anything the Lord had to say to him and wondered if there was some kind of response he was supposed to make to the preaching. So, although it was not something he would often choose to do, he decided to ask the Lord for a sign.

That day he and his family were due to leave on vacation. Before they left, he prayed silently, "Lord, if someone mentions the word *Korea* today, then I will respond to the sense of the burden being laid on me yesterday and know it was from Your hand." Then he got in the car to leave, feeling quite safe, since he knew he would not see anyone from his congregation for at least two weeks!

They spent the first night of their holiday with another former classmate. Willie casually told him of his unusual experience, carefully avoiding any mention of the name of a specific country. But before he could get very far into the story, his friend began to tease him and laughed, "Willie, maybe the Lord is sending you to Korea!"

When Willie himself was telling us the story later, sitting in the living room of his new apartment in Pusan, Korea, he told us that he remembered feeling that you could have knocked him over with a feather! Here were his orders to pursue the matter.

God Works at Both Ends

But there was another piece to the puzzle that he only discovered much later. During his first month in Korea, there was a knock at the door. Our friend had already met a number of Korean ministers, but the man who introduced himself was a complete stranger. He came straight to the point: would this new missionary please teach him and some of his friends how to do expository preaching?

Willie politely explained that the Mission required two years of orientation before he could really engage in independent work of that kind. Though he did not say so, he was amazed at the request, because he did not know that any of the Koreans were aware that this was indeed the very reason for which he had finally decided the Lord was calling him to their country. Thus he was most reluctant to refuse.

His visitor, however, would not take no for an answer. "But," he pleaded, "we have been praying for a long time for someone with these skills. Surely you could teach us! We started praying especially in . . . ," and he named the precise month when the burden had come down on Willie.

Needless to say, since that time, several hundred Korean pastors have taken seminars from that country preacher from Scotland who could not ignore the hand of his God upon him!

Do you see the interaction of the human and divine in this story? God desired His church in Korea to have a specific blessing, and a group of pastors moved another pastor thousands of miles by their prayer! Had it not been part of the divine plan, it would never have happened. But at the same time, the prayers had real power, because that is how the plan works out.

A Mystery

Clearly we are faced with a mystery. Here is contemporary evidence that there is indeed a connection between the two truths with which we began: God on the throne working all things after the counsel of His will, and insignificant Jabez praying down blessing that changed the history of his life. Yet who can say they really understand the connection? Nobody!

But think of it this way. We do not understand the Trinity, or how the two natures of Christ fit together in one person, but we still believe it. It is the same here. We do not understand exactly how God's sovereignty fits together with the human responsibility to pray, but we know they are both taught in Scripture. It is a valid position to say that we hold them both to be true and deny neither.

What we have done so far is see that God's sovereignty does not rule out the value of praying. We can genuinely bring our specific needs before His throne, anticipating divine intervention on earth. On the other hand, God never becomes subordinate to the desires of those He has created. Such a God would not be worthy of our allegiance. His will remains eternally constant.

The Divine Initiative

Two things, however, are quite clear about the connection and harmony of these two related truths. We have already looked at the first in some detail. As a means of accomplishing His sovereign plan, God has specifically chosen to use the prayers of His saints (which they base on His written Word) for His name to be glorified and His will to be done.

There is, however, a second factor that we can be sure of as we consider the fact that there has to be a connection between an eternal decree and an effectual prayer. In the prayers of His people, as everywhere else, our God has the initiative. This is very encouraging if we grasp what it means! Effective prayers start in heaven and are sent down to us by God Himself.

When God wants to begin working out one of His decrees, He apparently burdens one of His saints to pray just as He did with the Korean pastors. Sometimes, as the case may be before a real spiritual revival, He lays the burden on many at the same time. Thus when believers begin praying, the predestined blessing can be released. Conversely, when we do not pray, we will not have these blessings. So, the epistle of James says, "You do not have because you do not ask" (James 4:2).

This initiative of God in the prayers of His people, operating as the forerunner of His predestinated blessings on the world, works like this. The risen Christ is interceding for us in heaven (see Hebrews 7:24–28). The Spirit is there with Him, because the Father and the Son and the Holy Spirit are always together. And that same Spirit "also helps us in our weaknesses. For we do not know what we should pray for as we ought, but the Spirit Himself makes intercession for us with groanings which cannot be uttered" (Romans 8:26).

The Spirit leaves the throne where Jesus is praying and comes down into the believer's heart where He begins to reecho the intercessions of Jesus. It is as though the Holy

Spirit places a mirror inside our hearts and turns it in such a direction that it reflects back to heaven the deepest desires of the interceding Christ.

B. M. Palmer eloquently describes this prayer relationship between the Christian and his Savior and the Holy Spirit.

> It is the effectual, fervent prayer of the righteous man [that] prevails. But what renders prayer "effectual"? Not its length, nor its vehemence, nor its eloquence, nor its passion, but simply the living sympathy which is established between the soul pleading in the closet, and the Saviour interceding in the heavens.

> This is secured through the intervention of the Divine Spirit. He takes the desires which are in the heart of Jesus Christ, and works them into our hearts so that they become our desires. He takes the plea which is upon the lips of the great Advocate above, and seals it upon our lips as our prayer in Christ's blessed name. It is this sweet, but secret, correspondence between our Head and ourselves that makes true prayer at all. Aside from this, all is mere posture and the mutter of incantations.

> When the Holy Spirit thus pleads in the lower court of the believer's soul, what is it but the echo of the pleading in the higher court above? The voice on earth mingles with the voice in heaven, in the joint pleading for the gift of eternal life. How else shall we interpret the classical passage in Romans 8:26. . . . Have we then two intercessors? Yes, verily; but not divergent and clashing. They are the two comforters — the one and the other — both converging their distinct offices to one result. The one intercedes for us, the other intercedes *within* us.

> His work . . . [consists in] bringing the intercession of our Lord above, into the desires and petitions of the

Christian below; whereby they become the intercessions of the Spirit, who thus blends his advocacy with that of Christ himself.[9]

The Holy Spirit Influences Our Prayer

The Holy Spirit has a profound and varied ministry to us in this whole area. On occasion, God's presence is so overwhelming that all the believer can do is groan and weep. We sense we are being led to pray. We are aware of a pressing need, but either we cannot really pinpoint the exact problem, or we do not know what to ask the Lord to do about it.

Sometimes, the only fixed point in our prayer is the desire for God to have the glory. We find ourselves saying, "Lord, take over; Lord, work; Lord, do it," hardly able to formulate a whole sentence. We may even find ourselves praising God in an apparently hopeless situation which, on the face of it, should reduce us to tears.

My wife found herself in this very situation when she was facing a miscarriage one summer. She told me later that as I was driving her to the hospital in the middle of the night, she turned to the Lord to begin to pray, but instead of weeping, as she had expected, all she found she could do was praise him!

Lying in the back seat of the car, she did not experience the panic that she had always feared would descend at the threat of losing a baby. Instead, she had an overwhelming sense of God's love — a very special gift to her at that time. His presence came down, and her heart was filled with praise, for she knew that she could safely leave everything in His hands.

The Holy Spirit also helps us in prayer by making up for our weakness and for our ignorance of God's plan for some situation. But when we genuinely desire to pray according to God's will, we can be sure that the Holy Spirit is taking our deficient requests and then purging and reshaping them, until they are acceptable to the Father.

Remember that He takes what Jesus is praying for, and makes us pray for it. That is how our intercessions reecho the intercessions of the great High Priest who appears in heaven for us. Then the secret will, known to the great High Priest and to the Father, is reechoed in some way in our praying by the Spirit who comes from the Father and the Son. This explains how our praying on the basis of the revealed will begins to get into line with the secret will.

Our Prayer Activates the Eternal Plan

When we seek to be faithful to all that Scripture tells us of God's purposes on the one hand, and the evidence that prayer can be effectual, on the other, we have to conclude that the teachings are not, after all, contradictory. There is an influence of the spiritual world upon human personality, hand in hand with a consequent influence of human personality upon the spiritual world. The Holy Spirit moved the group of Christians in Korea to bring a specific need to the throne. They did so. Then the same Spirit moved the man, specifically chosen and prepared by God, halfway around the world.

The point is this: the infinite, personal God has purposes for His kingdom on earth that are shaped by His personal love for His creation. What a sense of security this should provide for us! Far from being discouraged from prayer by the existence of these unchanging decrees, we should be greatly motivated by the realization that they are designed to bring in His kingdom for us to enjoy. Furthermore, it has been the prayers of His people that have set the plan in motion throughout history.

For example, think of the election of sinners to salvation. This is certainly a matter far above our human minds. Nevertheless, we can grasp this much: there is a definite connection between people becoming burdened so that they pray much for someone they know who is lost, and then that lost person getting saved. Why? Like Jabez, who was "more honorable than his brothers," burdened, compassionate believers ask God for the soul of some lost sinner, and God gives them that soul. Why does He do it? Is it not because He is working out in time His eternal decrees and thus has burdened His saints to pray for this particular lost sheep in order to effectuate their election?

What an encouragement to pray, and indeed to pray without ceasing, for even the meanest and most hopeless men and women and youth! If you are praying for some lost member of your family, or even for an enemy, do not stop praying; your prayer may be the very means to unleash the divinely intended blessing in that person's soul.

This is an area where Korean Christians emphatically do not require any assistance from anywhere else. They understand this truth well. In fact, they have a great deal to teach the rest of the church, because one feature of their congregational life is the stress on congregational prayer for the spread of the gospel and other needs. And what struck us, when we visited there in 1989, was the seriousness and fervency of many of these prayer meetings.

Though there has only been real freedom for Christians for about twenty-five years, church members now number approximately 40 percent of the country's population.

Much of this phenomenal growth must be attributed to the fact that all-night prayer meetings are a regular feature on the churches' calendars and are attended by a large proportion of the membership. In addition, some rural churches still follow the pattern, established by the first Korean Christians, of gathering early every morning as well!

When you think about prayer, you may well ask, "Why should a sovereign God choose someone as weak as I, to carry out His decrees?" In response, we have to say that we cannot know precisely why. That is the kind of thing that will only be explained when we reach heaven. However, in the meantime, if that is the way He chooses to get precious souls saved, then our responsibility is not to speculate as to the reason but to act in accordance with His will!

"Asking Is the Rule of the Kingdom"

We should waste no time in getting down on our knees in prayer in order to release pent-up, divine blessing on multitudes in the devil's clutches. Where you have people actually praying for the lost, you find the lost being saved. That should be motivation enough to make us praise God, close this book, and begin praying!

May our hearts be encouraged to well up with fruitful prayers as we fill them with long thoughts of the profound connection between a sovereign God, on His all-controlling throne, and a humble Jabez on a little farm, bringing down life-changing blessing by prevailing prayer.

Let Charles H. Spurgeon have the last word:

> It is well said that "asking is the rule of the kingdom." It
> is a rule that will never be altered in anybody's case. If

the royal and divine Son of God cannot be exempted from the rule of asking that He may have, you and I cannot expect to have the rule relaxed in our favor.

God will bless Elijah and send rain on Israel, but Elijah must pray for it. If the chosen nation is to prosper, Samuel must plead for it. If the Jews are to be delivered, Daniel must intercede. God will bless Paul, and the nations shall be converted through him, but Paul must pray. Pray he did, without ceasing; his epistles show that he expected nothing except by asking for it. [10]

PART 2

WHY PRAY?

Give us this day our daily bread.
And forgive us our debts,
as we forgive our debtors.
And lead us not into temptation,
but deliver us from evil.
(Matthew 6:11-13)

4

PRAYER CHANGES US

A s the famous John Knox lay dying in Edinburgh in
the year 1572, he exclaimed to one of the elders
gathered around his bed, "I have been in meditation these
two last nights upon the troubled Kirk [church] of God,
despised of the world, but precious in his sight; and have
called to God for it, and commended it to Christ her head.
I have been fighting against Satan, who is ever ready to
assault. I have fought against spiritual wickednesses, and
have prevailed. I have been in heaven, where presentlie I
am, and tasted of the heavenly joys."[1]

This was the culmination of a life given for his Lord in
the service of his church and country, ending as it had
begun. For from earliest days, his prayers had been for the
success of the reformation of the church in Scotland, and
this desire shaped all the events of his life.

We can see from his dying words the power he had
won in the heavenly realm. But this ability to fight and
win in genuine spiritual warfare had not come without ex-
treme personal cost. His greatness and authority in prayer
came, in part, from the disciplines of suffering that the
Lord laid on him as a young man, at that time working as
a tutor to the sons of a nobleman in St. Andrews.

Soon after he began to be recognized as an outstanding expositor of the Scriptures, the French Army, in support of the Catholic Queen Regent of Scotland, attacked the town in retaliation for the murder of a cruel and repressive Cardinal. Knox, among others, was taken prisoner, and then spent nineteen dreadful months as a slave chained to an oar in a French galley.

In the summer of 1548, the ship he was in sailed close to his native land. He was desperately ill, probably with dysentery or typhoid, and had been unchained and left in the hold to die. But a friend propped him up so he could look across the waves toward St. Andrews.

Recognizing the steeple of the church where he first preached, and with his desire for the spread of the gospel still uppermost in his mind, he whispered, "I am fully persuaded how weak soever I appear, that I shall not depart this life till that my tongue shall glorify His godly name in the same place."[2] And, of course, he did.

Further periods of enforced exile from his beloved Scotland were the occasions of building up his understanding of the Reformation movement. First he spent several years among leading Anglican reformers in the evangelical court of Edward VI. Then later, when the ecclesiastical climate in England changed, forcing him to move again, he spent several more with Calvin in Geneva.

The Source of His Power

What better schools could he have attended in preparation for the monumental task God had for him in Scotland? Surely, the realization that God had directed his path would later supersede the grief of being far from home during those years. Yet at the time it would no doubt have forced him regularly to his knees in urgent intercession for the church there.

We think of him primarily as one of the greatest and most influential preachers and theologians of all time. He has even gone down in history as a powerful political figure. Yet, as we look at his final words, we see something maybe we would otherwise overlook: above all, he knew how to wrestle blessing from God in prayer. This is surely the secret of his incredible success.

But we can also say that his power with God in prayer was won through his faithfulness in hardship as well as because of the sanctifying work of the Holy Spirit through his suffering. Put another way, there was a direct correlation between his authority in prayer and his spiritual maturity. We can say that, in one sense, prayer not only changed history, but it changed John Knox!

His life is a very dramatic illustration of how God is always doing things inside His people to get them ready to receive more power and responsibility in prayer. This matter of maturity is the heart of the actual practice of prayer and is absolutely necessary before individuals — or indeed the church as a whole — can receive greater power.

Whenever we consider for ourselves the question of intercession (prayer for others), we very soon become aware of the need for "prayer power." This awareness alone should motivate us to consider carefully what it will take for each one of us to have the kind of influence that Knox had on his deathbed when we come to the end of our lives.

Prayer and God's People

As we have sought to understand the basic principles of prayer by looking at the example Jesus gave us, we have discovered that the first component of prayer is Godward. Now we are ready to make the transition into the second or "manward" part of His prayer, which deals directly with the needs of His people: "Give us this day our daily bread. And forgive us our debts, as we forgive our debtors. And do not lead us into temptation, but deliver us from the evil one " (Matthew 6:11–13).

While it is right to think about our own needs and lay them out before the Father, notice how Jesus says not "my" daily bread, "my" debts, nor deliver "me" from evil, but "our" and "us." Calvin rightly comments, in one of his sermons on 2 Samuel, that this teaches us to pray together, as the whole body of Christ, in harmony with one another and with compassion for one another. Thus, the second part of the Lord's Prayer directs our attention to the Lord's people and their life and service together in this world, something that we as Christians should take seriously. At his death, John Knox's thoughts transcended his own concerns. He spent his last moment in prayer for others. We need to see that part of the commandment to love our neighbor as ourselves can be fulfilled in just this way.

What is God doing in our lives to make us mighty in prayer and so fulfill the ultimate purpose of glorifying His name? From one point of view we can consider the whole process of maturing in the Christian life as God at work in us in order to get us to the position where He can trust us with ever greater prayer power.

Leaving Toys Behind

Recently I was visiting a community in North Carolina where I first ministered after my ordination in 1968. As I met people I had not seen in eight or nine years, it struck me that I was observing a kind of parable of the way God works in the lives of His people.

Little boys, who had been playing with cap-pistols then, are now running their father's farm or have important positions in the bank. As they have matured, instead of giving them toys and candy, their parents are able to turn over plantations to them! That is why when I saw one of them twenty years later, he had full charge of a large and busy plantation, with several families dependent on his management for their livelihood.

Why was there a change? Because he had developed sufficiently well by age thirty to be able to handle responsibility and power, something he could not have done at age eleven.

Similarly prayer power requires maturity. As we mature and receive more power, God receives more glory. In other words, we must always remember that although the second part of the Lord's Prayer deals with *our* needs, it is nevertheless a means for fulfilling the first part, namely, bringing glory to God, hallowing His name.

The better the young farmers in North Carolina handled greater cares as grown men, the more honor they reflected upon their parents. So it is with us in the Christian life. As we mature over the years, God can entrust us with more power and authority in prayer. The more blessing we bring down through prayer, the more God is glorified.

How God Develops Maturity in Us

In order to appreciate the divinely ordained connection between life and prayer, we must examine the meaning of spiritual maturity and what it accomplishes in the realm of prayer.

We must never forget that maturity is the goal of all that God is allowing to happen in our Christian lives. He wants us to be all that we can be. The key to His dealings with us is given in Romans 8:28–30:

> And we know that all things work together for good to those who love God, to those who are the called according to His purpose. For whom He foreknew, He also predestined to be conformed to the image of His Son, that He might be the firstborn among many brethren. Moreover whom He predestined, these He also called; whom He called, these He also justified; and whom He justified, these He also glorified.

This passage, and the whole context in which it is found, teaches that the ultimate purpose of the entire plan of God is to make us more like the Lord Jesus Christ. It is rooted in predestination and consummated in glorification. And these are both linked together by justification, new birth, sanctification, and all the other steps of the salvation process. Specifically, what Romans 8:28 is saying in asserting that all things work together for good is that God takes everything that happens in our individual lives (and in the whole historical experience of His church) and works it together to shape us into the image of His blessed Son.

Suffering Can Be Good for You!

We have all come across the point of view espoused by many popular preachers today known as "prosperity theology." There is a serious flaw in this teaching, because — contrary to its assertions — the ultimate good for me, and for God's people in general, is not a better job, good health, or a fabulous house, car, or new yacht! That is sim-

ply wishful thinking. God does indeed give wonderful
gifts to His children, but the ultimate good for us all is to
be like Jesus.

In fact, even those things that are listed in Romans 8:35,
38, and 39 and which, from the human perspective, are indeed terrible: tribulation, distress, persecution, famine,
nakedness, peril, sword, death, principalities, powers, height,
and depth are deliberately allowed by God into our lives. He
has planned each one, in His loving, beneficent purposes for
us, as a way of shaping us into the image of Jesus.

As communism tightened its grip on China in the
1940s, Christians experienced persecution and danger.
Years later, the following poem was found scribbled on
the flyleaf of the Bible of an unknown missionary, believed to have been martyred during that time. "Prosperity
theology" would have held little credibility with this
Christian, who had learned to see the presence of God in
the hard times.

Although lacking in polish, it nevertheless expresses
beautifully the assurance of God's hand at work in our lives.

THE SCULPTOR

A block of marble silent stood
Before the sculptor where He would.
He smote with steady hand well skilled
And thus with blow on blow, fulfilled
The vision of his mind.

At first with chisel coarse and stroke
Unspared, the corners off he broke.
And soon the form appeared.
And then, with finer tools he wrought,
And finer yet, until he brought
The perfect image forth.

So, with unerring skillfulness,
With cunning hand and sure,
'Tis as the marble groweth less
The likeness groweth more.

So God divinely works with those
He, in the eternal ages chose,
To show His work of grace,
And thus with blow on blow to trace
The image of His Son!
How blest to know, that He who holds
His tools, before His eyes beholds
His own beloved One!

The cares and sorrow day by day,
The troubles that o'ershade the way
Together, work for good;
And nothing e'er by chance befalls
The one whom God, in purpose calls,
In whom His love is found.

And when we have the glory gained,
And Christ's full image have attained,
We'll praise His sovereign grace,
And bless the hand that dealt each blow,
Upon the marble here below
In working out His will.

The author surely would have been no exception to the
fact that none of us welcome suffering, because it genuinely hurts us and does not necessarily feel like a "spiritual
experience"! It may even feel exactly the opposite! God
may seem notably absent. Yet this servant of God had discovered the truth of Romans 8 and was to find Him trust-
worthy even in death.

Maturity Gives Power in Prayer

Consider what this process of increasing conformity to the incarnate Son of God accomplishes in the realm of prayer. In John 11:42 Jesus says, "And I know that you always hear Me." He knew His prayers to His heavenly Father were effective. This means that the more like Jesus *we* become, the more our asking becomes like His asking. In medieval paintings, exceptionally godly men and women are always depicted with halos of light around their heads. The artists were expressing visually the fact that their subjects were filled with the light of God and stood out from the crowd because they had become like Christ, the Holy One.

When we are like Him, we will be different, and it will make our prayers different, too. The more our character is like Jesus', then the more our praying is like His praying. Thus when we pray, God hears the voice of His beloved Son ringing through our prayers. And of course, He always answers the prayers of Jesus.

This reality explains one whole line of New Testament teaching on prayer, which otherwise seems difficult for the human mind to comprehend. In other words, there are in the New Testament several absolute assurances that God will answer prayer, if we ask in simple faith. Yet in the same New Testament, there are other passages which contain another line of teaching about prayer which is conditional.

By examining each line of teaching, we will attempt to see how they fit together in light of what we are learning about how God is at work in the lives of His people.

Straightforward Promises

First look at Mark 11:22-24:

So Jesus answered and said to them, "Have faith in God. For assuredly, I say to you, whoever says to this mountain, 'Be removed, and be cast into the sea,' and does not doubt in his heart, but believes that those things he says will come to pass, he will have whatever he says. Therefore I say to you, whatever things you ask when you pray, believe that you receive them, and you will have them."

Now, turn to John 14:13–14:

"And whatever you ask in My name, that I will do, that the Father may be glorified in the Son. If you ask anything in My name, I will do it."

He then goes on to speak of the need to love Him and keep His commandments. And a little later, He continues in 15:7:

"If you abide in Me, and My words abide in you, you will ask what you desire, and it shall be done for you."

Notice also John 16:23–24:

"And in that day you will ask Me nothing. Most assuredly, I say to you, whatever you ask the Father in My name He will give you. Until now you have asked nothing in My name. Ask, and you will receive, that your joy may be full."

Finally, turn to 1 John 5:14–15:

Now this is the confidence that we have in Him, [Jesus], that if we ask anything according to His will, He hears us. And if we know that He hears us, whatever we ask, we know that we have the petitions that we have asked of Him.

Here then are some of the straightforward promises about asking and receiving. They have a particular appeal to our modern society, with its orientation toward instant gratification. One can certainly understand the attraction of prosperity theology! But there is also a line of equally inspired New Testament teaching on prayer which is definitely conditional.

At first glance this seems to be contradictory. On the one hand He clearly said, "ask [in simple faith] and you will receive it." But then "the red tape" appears! That is the last thing we want to hear. When things are tough, we want instant relief.

Have you ever received a large envelope in the mail, with the phrase, "OPEN IMMEDIATELY — YOU COULD BE THE LUCKY WINNER OF MILLIONS!" in large red letters on the outside? Maybe the first time one of those comes to your house, you open it hopefully. But you do not have to read very far before you notice something written in small print at the bottom of the page! Those are the conditions that put limits on the offer.

What is the "small print" in the case of prayer? Is there any, and if so, can anyone hope to qualify? Or is it as far out of reach as the promise of millions?

The Small Print

When we look at the promises that encourage us that our prayers will be answered, we do indeed discover that some of them are conditional. They will only be fulfilled after *continual asking*. There are absolute promises about answering the prayer of simple faith side by side with promises which require some other condition to be fulfilled be-

fore the prayer can be heard. How can both kinds of promises fit together? Are they really contradictory?

There is a whole line of teaching in the Old and the
New Testaments that offers some solution. We know that
many of the people whose lives are recorded in Scripture
had to struggle for a long time. Look at those instances
where continual asking, wrestling, and struggling brought
success. (We will also take a more practical look at the
subject in Chapter Seven.)

- Isaiah speaks of our giving the Lord "no rest . . . till He
  makes Jerusalem a praise in the earth" (62:7).

- In the New Testament, Christ tells the parable of the persistent widow who kept coming back to the unjust judge
  over and over again. The Lord said that our prayer has to
  be like that, coming back and pressing on until we receive the answer (see Luke 18:1–8).

- He also speaks of the bold friend who, at midnight, kept
  asking a neighbor for bread. He came to the other man's
  house at an inconvenient hour of the night and kept beating on the door until he got what he wanted (Luke 11:5–
  8).

- We see this same battling in Abraham's prayer for
  Sodom: "Would You also destroy the righteous with the
  wicked? Suppose there were fifty righteous within the
  city?" (Genesis 18:23–24). He eventually reduced his
  condition from fifty to forty-five to forty to thirty then
  twenty, and finally came down to ten. "Suppose ten
  should be found there?" And God said, "I will not destroy it for the sake of ten (verse 32)." Yet even that condition could not be met, which meant that Sodom was
  burned. However, Abraham's pleading did have some effect. Because of his prayers, the angels warned his

nephew Lot so that he and his two daughters were delivered from the flames (see Genesis 18 and 19).

- The Old Testament also tells of Daniel's prolonged struggling and fasting for three weeks, entreating God for forgiveness and restoration for Israel (see Daniel 10).

- Similarly, the Apostle Paul gives glimpses all through his letters of his own wrestling in prayer. When he wrote to the church he had founded in Galatia, he described himself as laboring "in birth . . . until Christ is formed in you" (Galatians 4:19). Giving birth to a baby is by no means an easy or trouble-free event! Paul's prayer for their growth took supreme effort!

- And then finally, there is the gospel account of our Lord Jesus Christ himself. The perfect God-man stands in our place, wrestling in prayer for victory in the Garden of Gethsemane. He is pleading and struggling with the Father, because He faces becoming so absolutely identified with the sins of His people that He will become blackened by their sins and for a time be cut off from the divine presence.

  Prayer, for Jesus, was neither easy nor automatic. He knew experientially how much struggle it involved. As He faced entering into our hell, He fought in prayer until He reached the place where He could say: "If this is the only way Your name can be hallowed in the salvation of My people, 'Your will be done'" (see John 17).

Now all of these passages have a common theme. The Bible never hides the struggling, wrestling, and uncertain nature of many experiences of prayer. It gives us at the same time absolute assurance that God will answer prayer, coupled with the warning that there is a conditional side to intercession.

We must not lose sight of the fact that there are indeed *absolute* promises — "you ask and you will have it." But Scripture tell us "up front" that there are also prayers that are not answered right away. No doubt we have already found out for ourselves that some kinds of prayer require time and struggle. Even the great father of the faith, Abraham, had to adjust his request as he pled with God to withhold judgment. If he had encountered difficulty, we can surely expect the same!

Jesus wants us to be aware of that side of prayer. There is a sense in which He says to us, "If you *keep* coming back, and *only if you keep coming back*; . . . if you *keep* knocking, if you *keep* seeking. . . . But if you quit knocking and if you quit seeking, you will not get it."

So we do indeed have both kinds of promises, conditional and absolute. How do they fit together?

Spiritual Maturity Resolves the Contradiction

Do you remember the little boy who prayed for slides for everyone? God did not answer his prayer because the child had a great deal to learn. He was right to count on the fact that God has indeed promised to answer prayer. But he had not yet discovered the truth that our asking needs to be in accordance with God's will for the blessing to be given.

Now this creates problems for us in that it is hard for us to be quite sure that our requests are in line with His purposes. The key to our dilemma is found in passages such as John 15:7: "*If* you abide in Me, and My words abide in you, you will ask what you desire, and it shall be done for you " (emphasis added). The first part is not so much a condition as a context for prevailing prayer.

In other words, the kind of asking that immediately gets through comes from the one who is abiding in Christ and whose desires are shaped in accordance with the words of Jesus in Scripture. This is not just any kind of asking but is asking in Christ, or as it says in 1 John 5:14: "if we ask anything *according to His will*, He hears us" (emphasis added).

If these things are true, and if we want power in prayer, then the most important question we can raise is: "How shall you and I reach the place where we 'ask according to His will'?" It is by abiding in Him and having His authoritative, gracious, transforming words abide in us.

Now we are in a position to begin to understand the "small print." God is working throughout our whole life to make us like His Son. He lets us be hurt and breaks us down. The heavenly Sculptor chips away at our personalities and our lives. All the while we keep praying. Then He builds us up and encourages us, and His Word takes deeper root in us. At last, from the deepest part of our being, we want what the Son wants. Along the way, our prayers are transformed, too. The condition of abiding in Jesus is met, and our prayers are answered, "for the Father hears Him always."

We already know from Romans 8:26–27 that the Holy Spirit enters the believer and helps him or her to pray by reechoing the intercessions of Christ in heaven. But there is an effect in our lives beyond just the straightforward matter of taking time out to pray, having our "quiet time," or covering our prayer list. Sometimes the cross has to be applied in daily experience; we have to pass through many disciplines so that we can mature to the point of being genuinely receptive to the Holy Spirit's echoing of the intercessions of Christ within us. That is why praying through to success may take so long.

God at Work in Us to Change Us

Only recently a friend told us of an experience which illustrates beautifully how prayer changes us so that the precise prayer is actually less important than what God is doing in our lives.

Judy, an attractive and vivacious Christian, has a lovely singing voice and has often been asked to minister in various settings. But six months ago, a doctor found some growths in her larynx which could possibly become malignant. Surgery was recommended.

Dreading the thought of having to stop talking, she put it off as long as possible! The existence of the growth was not nearly so worrying to her as the necessity for hospitalization and then the enforced inability to communicate. Daily she prayed that the Lord would give her the grace to handle the operation and the period of recovery.

What a struggle she found it! Over and over she begged, "Please, just help me learn to be happy about conforming to Your will. I don't know how I can face not being able to talk, with my family responsibilities and the fact that I love to be around people!"

Although she is a gifted musician, she told us that she had always been rather reluctant to agree to perform. Suddenly she started to see that her talent was indeed a gift from God and that He really had a purpose in giving it to her. Then it became particularly precious, and she began to pray that there would still be opportunities in the future for her to sing for Him.

Eventually the day came for the presurgery checkup. The doctor, also a friend of ours, examined her throat to identify the exact location of the growths in preparation for the procedure. Then he stopped and consulted his files, and looked again. "There is nothing there any more!" he exclaimed in amazement. All her fears were over!

She rushed home to tell her husband. His reply surprised her almost as much as the doctors report. Unknown to her he had prayed every day that the Lord would heal her, while she had never once thought of such a prayer! Yet God had not only healed her, but had radically changed her attitudes about many things.

She was unspeakably grateful to be healed, but what delighted her even more was how God the Holy Spirit had directed her prayers so that her whole attitude to her musical talent was changed. She knew that she had come out of the difficult experience more conformed to His will.

God is doing something big inside praying people. He is not primarily interested in our coming one by one as single, solitary individuals, asking for certain things, receiving them, and then going off by ourselves and remaining unchanged during the whole process. God will not have that, because He is far more interested in *us* than in what we ask — although that does certainly interest Him.

Instead God is working to *change us* through our asking, through all that He allows to come into our lives, through the Scriptures, through the Holy Spirit, through the providences, the hard things, the hurtful things, and the happy things. He is active in all these things to shape us into the likeness of Jesus, so that we will be at the place where the Holy Spirit is able to intercede, work, and plead inside us, reflecting the tones of the voice of Jesus.

Ultimately, it is not so much what we ask, but *who we are when we pray* that counts the most. Well, who are we when we pray "in Jesus' name"?

United to Christ

We have spoken of the necessity of "abiding in Christ" (see John 15). But how can we do that when we are here on earth and He seems to be so far distant from us in heaven?

In the first place, God never leaves His people alone. But more specifically, when Jesus was speaking to His disciples before His death, although He was going back to the Father in His glorified body, He said, "I will not leave you orphans; I will come to you. . . . Abide in Me, and I in you" (John 14:18; 15:4). Another way of describing His presence in us is to say that we are *united to Christ.*

"Union with Christ" is something we do not hear preached very often, and yet nothing could be more important for our prayer life. Why should just knowing about this truth make so much difference to powerful prayer?

The answer is simple. Realizing who I am in Jesus sets my faith free to pray those kinds of victorious prayers which overcome the world! Is it any wonder that the devil does not want you to realize just who you are in Christ?

Spiritual Understanding

Some of you whose memory goes back to the 1940s and 1950s will recall the once popular cartoon character "Mr. Magoo." On Saturday afternoons at the cinema, how we enjoyed seeing Mr. Magoo—who was extremely near-sighted—lose his glasses! He would crawl around some impressive corporate or government office, constantly knocking things over onto the heads of self-important people, or perhaps mistake a policeman for a hat-rack, much to the delight of the audience which roared with childish laughter.

Now the devil wants to make us lose our spiritual glasses, so that — like old Mr. Magoo — we will be at a total loss as to what is actually going on around us. He wants us to live as "spiritual myopics," who can barely see to the end of our noses when it comes to understanding the kind of victorious faith that overcomes the world through prayer. Or to put it more plainly, if he can keep you from knowing who you are in union with Jesus Christ, he can largely neutralize your arsenal of faith-empowered prayer, which he fears so very much.

To realize afresh who you are in union with the victorious Son of God will get your feet on praying ground. Indeed, one of the main reasons the New Testament epistles were written was precisely so we could come to know who we really are in Christ. For example, look at Paul's prayer in Ephesians 1:15-23. There he asks the Lord to give the church members to whom he was writing "the spirit of wisdom and revelation in the knowledge of [Christ]" so that "the eyes of [their] understanding being enlightened," they could know the hope of His calling, the riches of their inheritance, and the greatness of His resurrection power available to them. Once they became aware of these things which were given to them in union with Christ, Paul knew they would be set free to take up the weapon of prayer (see Ephesians 6:18).

Becoming aware of who you are in Jesus Christ is at least as wonderful as some poor orphan finding out that he is the lost son of a wealthy family, who perhaps was kidnapped years before but now has been traced down by them so they can take him home to a fabulous mansion, loving relatives, and wealth untold. How this would change his attitude! And what God the Father has done for us lost sinners is more, not less, marvelous than this, as Paul shows us in Ephesians 2.

But what we too often forget, much to the detriment of our prayer lives, is Paul's constant emphasis that everything the Father has for us can only be received when we are living on the basis of union with Christ, His beloved Son (see Romans 6; 1 Corinthians 15; Galatians 5; Ephesians 1and 2).

If union with Christ is really this important for prayer — and for everything else in the Christian life — then it is no waste of time to ask just what it means in good, practical terms. This matter of who we really are (for instance, when we begin to pray) can be understood in terms of ancestry or of a family tree.

Family Trees

I spoke earlier of an orphan who one day realized he came from a wealthy family and that he was returning to them. From that time on, everything was different. Because he discovered his real family tree, his blood ancestors, he had the right to move from one family to another.

There is a sense in which that is how it is with the man or woman who is in Christ. By faith he or she has literally been engrafted into a different family tree (see Romans 11:16–24). A Christian transfers from one family to another.

The Bible teaches that every person in the world is seen by God as being in only one of two possible family trees and nowhere else. As the Apostle Paul describes it,

every person is either "in Adam" or "in Christ;" or stated
in another way, everyone is either united to the first Adam
or the last Adam (see especially Romans 5:12-21 and 1
Corinthians 15:21–22; 45–49).

By birth, every man is born "in Adam." We inherit our
human nature from a fallen ancestor, so that what David
said of himself is true of us all: "Behold, I was brought
forth in iniquity, and in sin my mother conceived me"
(Psalm 51:5). As Paul says in Ephesians 2:3, we were "by
nature children of wrath." In the eyes of God our natural
background, our ancient family tree, is one of rebellion,
poverty, and wrath. That is why the ordinary unsaved person actually works desperately hard to flee from Him, instead of seeking the heavenly Father's face in loving
prayer (see Romans 1:18–32).

But in the new birth, when the Holy Spirit has
anointed our eyes so that we look upon Jesus Christ as
personal Lord and Savior, we become a new creation (see
2 Corinthians 5:17). This means that God takes us out of
the old stock (or family tree) of condemned, defeated
Adam, and grafts us into the new, resurrection stock, or
family tree, of the victorious Christ.

We are now in a gloriously different situation! In the
new family setting, all that Christ gained for us in His incarnate life, atoning death, and bodily resurrection is immediately available for us in accordance with our needs,
our faith, and the Lord's purposes.

Various aspects of this truth are described for us in
different parts of Scripture. First Corinthians 12:13 says
that we are baptized with the Holy Spirit into the body of
Christ. Romans 6:3–5 says that we are baptized into union
with Christ in both His death and His resurrection.

John 15:1–8, to which we have already referred, is another way of stating the same thing. When it speaks of our "abiding in Christ" just as the branches abide in the grapevine, it is a picture of our union with Him. Thus His life flowing through us is like vital sap so that we bear fruit, *His* fruit.

Finally, Galatians 5:22–23 describes the fruit of the Spirit which is produced in the personalities of those in union with Christ in this new family tree. Love, joy, peace, and so forth are the family characteristics.

The Holy Spirit makes this profound truth of the union of the believer with Christ absolutely real, although the "mechanics" of it far surpass the human understanding. Calvin once said that the Holy Spirit is able so to join things in heaven and things in earth, that the life, virtue, and knowledge of the one can be genuinely shared by the other.[3]

How can we be united to Christ and move permanently from one family to another? The bond of this union with Christ is faith. Again, in the words of Calvin, "faith unites man to God and makes God to dwell in man."[4]

Chosen by the Father to be engrafted by the Spirit and bonded by faith into His Son, we have an incredibly happy, new family identity: we are united to Christ! How different our prayers are when we kneel down with an awareness of who we are and what we have in Christ!

Accepted in the Beloved

There are tremendous implications of our being united to Christ for the subject of prayer. The first is that we are made acceptable to the Father, and thus meet a vital re-

quirement of the "small print." We pray in His name and
get right through to God.

During a communicants class, the minister encouraged
the young people to come to the Lord's table with a particular hymn in their mind. It included the lines:

> Look, Father, look on His anointed face
> And only look on us as found in Him;
> Look not on our misusings of Thy grace,
> Our prayer so languid and our faith so dim:
> For lo! between our sins and their reward
> We set the passion of Thy Son our Lord.

This was a wise choice, particularly as teenagers so
often are going through a time when they feel unaccept-
able to their parents, their peers, and even to themselves.
How could a holy God possibly accept them?

Part of the reason for their instability — though by no
means all of it — is the fact that they are often tossed by a
tumult of surging emotions as their hormones "gear up"
for adult life. In particular, their strong awareness of their
budding sexual drive can catch them off-guard.

As new and strange thoughts and urges cross their
minds, they wonder if they are sinning and often feel acute
shame. Of course, as we know, the mere fact of being
tempted is not sin. What is wrong is to welcome the temptation and to succumb to it. Of course, some may do exactly that, in which case they would be right to feel guilty!
Nevertheless, others who are genuinely committed to the
scriptural teaching on purity are so shocked by the force-
fulness and newness of their emotions that they are convinced they cannot be acceptable to God.

Their sense of guilt may be compounded by the fact
that we live in a highly sexually charged society where so

little is secret about adult behavior. This causes the teenagers to misinterpret their own experiences and take them
too seriously, because they do not have any other scale by
which to measure them. Even where some sin is involved,
often it takes on a far greater meaning in their minds than
is really justified. Some even think that because they are
unable to control their thoughts, they may as well give up
altogether.

How valuable to know that union with our Lord means
nothing can keep us from being heard by the Father. It
simply does not matter how we feel or how besieged we
are by temptation. We know that we can approach God's
throne by virtue of the fact that Christ faced and defeated
every temptation for us. This is what the hymn means. We
come *through* Him, and it is *His* life that God sees when
we seek refuge from our sins in Him.

His human life was the perfect response to the Father
in all these areas, so that our failures do not cut us off
from God when we are in Him. This substitution of His
holy life in place of our imperfect life, far from making us
careless in this or any other area, will hearten us to strive
all the more to reflect His purity.

Power in Prayer When We Are in Christ

Remember that Christ's historic life in our place in no
sense, of course, removes present struggle from us. After
all, "in the days of His flesh . . . [He] offered up prayers
and supplications, with vehement cries and tears," (Hebrews 5:7.) In order to win, He had to struggle in prayer
just as we do. Our power in prayer is predicated on His
success in that very place, because an essential part of His
victory over sin and death lay in the fact that He prayed.

This adds a new dimension as well as a new hope to the sufferings and difficulties in life that we have already have discovered are inescapable. They will change us into men or women who prevail in prayer, for we are praying in Christ, who suffered and died, but rose again. We are not alone and will ultimately win, as did our Savior.

Finally, it is particularly encouraging to realize that we get through to God because *He* was the one who chose us in Jesus. We were not the ones who chose Him. Yes, we are extremely weak and frail. But He knew exactly what was ahead when He called us. He knew our needs and therefore had ready all the resources of the God-man to offer us, full of life-giving and transforming power.

In summary, as we seek to trust God in Christ, follow His Word, and rely upon His Spirit, and as the Lord is using His providential control and care to grow us and mature us, then, more and more, the voice of His Son rings through our prayers. Thus we ask according to His will, and it shall be done for us. Through it all, we grow from the immature little lad, playing with toys in the shadow of his father's barn, into responsible adults, running plantations, earning a living and caring for others as well as ourselves.

This was how John Knox could enter the heavenly realm. The character of Christ had been so chiseled into him, and his life and prayers had been brought so much into accord with his master, that at the end of it all, he was able to see into the very place where Christ is now on His throne.

This long look at what God is doing in the lives of those whom He has placed in Christ prepares us to consider specifically the things for which Christ would have the members of His body pray.

Praying Scriptural Promises

In other words, just knowing that our lives are being transformed day by day is not enough! We still need to ask, "What can I do for my *praying* to become more like the praying of Jesus? How can I begin to move from the conditional to the absolute so that the voice of the Son really does ring through my prayers each day?"

John 15:7 gives us the clue: "If . . . My words abide in you, you will ask what you desire, and it shall be done for you." In other words, the promises of Scripture are to abide in us, so that from the inside out we plead these promises in prayer.

Even though the Holy Spirit has already brought us into vital union with Christ, we must still see to it that His words *abide* in us. In other words, the patterns of Scripture are to be the instruments that are allowed to shape our lives in a general way, and then when we begin specifically praying, we pray on the basis of these same inspired words.

When a blocked drain once caused rather severe water damage to our house, we had to check our insurance contract to see whether or not we could expect any compensation. Only after we were certain that we were indeed covered, did we call the agent, because then we could cite the terms we had originally agreed upon. The company, fortunately, had no choice but to pay for the repairs.

In a similar way, if we wish to know the kind of request God has committed Himself to answer, we can search through the Bible.

John Calvin uses another picture. He speaks of prayer as a means of using the promises of Scripture to enter the treasury of heaven: "There is nothing that we are promised to expect from the Lord, which we are not also bidden to ask of him in prayer. It is absolutely true that it is by prayer that we dig up the treasures that were pointed out by the Gospel of our Lord, and which our faith has gazed upon longingly."[5]

Similarly, Charles Spurgeon said: "Every promise of Scripture is a writing of God, which may be pleaded before Him with this reasonable request, 'Do as Thou hast said!' The Creator will not cheat the creature who depends upon his truth; and far more, the Heavenly Father will not break his word to his own child."[6]

So, in union with Christ, we pray according to His promises. Through it all we are seeking to live our life according to the pattern given to us in the Scriptures: that we have faith in God and express that faith by seeking to be obedient to His Word, all, of course, by the help of His Spirit who is given to us in the new birth.

Anyone who has learned to use a computer will remember the first few frustrating weeks when they were still unfamiliar with the correct commands and often could not figure out the right combination of keys to persuade the machine to fulfill a certain task. In somewhat the same way, we need to know the promises of God's Word to know what we can plead before Him. We could almost say, to change the metaphor slightly, that our minds need to be "programmed" according to the Bible!

Specific Requests

In the model prayer, Christ seems to summarize all the promises of Scripture into the three requests:

● Give us this day our daily bread.

● Forgive us our debts as we forgive our debtors.

● Lead us not into temptation but deliver us from the evil one.

Christ teaches His people to come together and ask their Father to give to the whole body: provision (bread), pardon, and protection. Remember that when we request these things of the Father, we are asking Him for something that Jesus said He is pleased to give us, however much Satan tries to tell us otherwise and discourage us from praying.

Provision

First, Christ teaches us to ask the Father for our daily bread. Above all, that means that it is legitimate for us to ask God to provide for our physical needs.

Mrs. Edith Schaeffer wrote in her biography of the Schaeffer family, *The Tapestry*, that when she and her husband were in seminary, a professor's wife rebuked her for praying for the Lord to send in needed money by saying: "In prayer we only ask for spiritual things."[7]

If that were the case, Jesus was certainly wrong to have told us to ask for daily bread! And the psalmist had it all wrong when he wrote: "I have been young, and now am old; yet I have not seen the righteous forsaken, nor his descendants begging bread" (Psalms 37:25). Something was amiss, also, in the inspiration of 3 John 2: "Beloved, I pray that you may prosper in all things and be in health, just as your soul prospers." Scripture does indeed have plenty to say about God providing for all of our daily, earthly needs. So there is no need to be at all embarrassed about praying for material things.

Once I was going fishing with a layman from a church in rural Mississippi. As we were riding in his pick-up truck down the dirt road to the pond, we were discussing prayer. I remarked to this kindhearted Christian that at times I was ashamed of asking God for money.

Now he was aware of the particularly difficult situation that I was in at the time. So he turned his head toward me and said simply and profoundly, "Yes, but you ain't got no other way to get it!" He knew that it is God's delight to grant us material things. It honors Him when we ask Him, and He is pleased with us for asking.

But of course we must remember that this second, manward part of the Lord's Prayer is the way of fulfilling the first part, which is "Hallowed be Your name." God does grant us material things, including health and financial prosperity, insofar as it is in accord with the glory of His name and the predestinated part we have to play in reflecting the glory of that name. As we grow closer to Christ and the Holy Spirit reechoes His intercessions within our souls, there is no doubt we will be led into the right balance. We will begin to discern which material things it is right for us to keep pleading for, but also which ones we can joyfully forget! Then we can say with George Mueller, "I have no will in the matter."[8]

Here was someone who knew what he was talking about! He was a most remarkable man of prayer who lived in the last century. He operated orphanages for hundreds of children in the west of England and his sole means of support was looking to God in prayer for provision.

On one occasion there was no milk for the children's breakfast. He had them take their places in the dining room as usual and told them to bow their heads and thank their heavenly Father that He was going to provide the milk they needed.

A few moments later, there was a knock at the door. A milk cart, on its way to make deliveries, and loaded with milk, had broken down right outside the orphanage. The driver asked if they would please take and use the milk, as it would sour before the cart could be repaired? What encouragement to prayer! No wonder Mueller was not ashamed to ask for material things. Yet he also had learned that power in prayer was not to be an end in itself. The fact is that the more we mature in union with Christ, the more we will be motivated to become more like Jesus, and the more loosely we will hold onto some of the legitimate material things.[9]

Furthermore, since Christ teaches us to pray not merely for *my* daily bread but for *our* daily bread, we are to be concerned for the material needs of the whole body of Christ, and indeed, like the good Samaritan, for our neighbor.

The closer we get to Christ, the more we will transcend our own immediate concerns and become burdened and full of compassion for the poor and oppressed across the earth. As Christ cares for and intercedes for others, we will do so as well — and we will intercede more for others, give more to others, and think less of self the nearer we draw to the great High Priest. As we mature in Christ, we will pray more and more, "Give us this day *our* daily bread."

Pardon

Next Jesus teaches all of His people to ask God to pardon their sins, as they forgive those who have sinned against them. What Jesus has in mind here is not so much that once-for-all, eternal pardon that the believer appropriates at conversion. That is the kind that we receive when we are justified by faith in Jesus' finished work on the cross through the grace of God. Rather He is dealing with the day to day need that we have, as justified but imperfectly sanctified sinners, of forgiveness and cleansing.

We are to confess our sins daily in the name of Jesus and thus appropriate forgiveness through His cleansing blood, (see 1 John 1–2). We need to ask others for forgiveness wherever and whenever possible (see Matthew 5:23ff.). Also we are to see to it that we have the kind of attitude that is prepared to forgive those who have hurt us. That is the way to prevent the growing and festering "root of bitterness," (Hebrews 12:15) which can destroy us and damage our relationship with others and with God.

Of course, such behavior does not come naturally to us! We are only able to do all of this because we abide in Christ and He lives in us. His forgiving spirit can triumph over our bitterness and resentment as we look to Him and mature in Him.

The fact that we forgive our debtors does not in any sense pay God to forgive us our debts. Not at all! It is the other way round. The Jesus whose blood cleanses all sin dwells in us and imparts His own forgiving attitude to us who have truly received His forgiveness and Him. In other words, we never receive God's forgiveness without receiving God Himself. The fact of God being within us and our abiding in Christ changes us into forgiving persons.

How many churches need to take this matter seriously, if they wish to have the kind of power in prayer which could transform a community! Only recently in a phone conversation, a friend was expressing to us her continual grief that there is one lady in their fellowship who refuses to talk to her because of some long-forgotten quarrel. How many times is this sad situation multiplied throughout our land, and how often is it the chief cause of the ineffectiveness of Christian ministries?

The fact is, the more we mature in Christ, the more we are possessed by love that "will cover a multitude of sins"(1 Peter 4:8). And then the more forgiving we are, the more power we can be trusted with in prayer, so that we grow from being ministered unto to ministering in His name to others.

Protection

Finally, Jesus teaches His people to pray for protection: "Lead us not into temptation, but deliver us from the evil one." This part of the prayer becomes increasingly meaningful to those of us with teenage children when we think of the hosts of potentially life-threatening temptations they may encounter in our modern, largely "post-Christian" society. We realize we need to pray in this way particularly for them — though it alerts us to the fact that there are specific temptations that can hit us also at mid-life and beyond!

The great Greek scholar A.T. Robertson felt that Calvin's interpretation of this petition was correct: namely, that we are asking the Lord to keep us from getting into situations of trial or temptation which would be stronger than we could resist.[10]

The Bible teaches that the devil *tempts* us, meaning that he encourages us to violate the moral standards which are, after all, based on God's own character. On the other hand, it also teaches that God Himself does *test* or *try* us. However, in His case, it is not with a view to degradation, but with a view to strengthening us by developing our trust in Him, building our own character, and increasing our ability to wage bigger battles for His kingdom.

It has been said that "God uses sin sinlessly!" He is in control even of the devil. Obviously, we have all experienced—to our dismay—that God does allow the devil to get at us. Yet God's purpose is to use these trials in which the evil one wants to degrade us as a way to build our Christian character. So Jesus tells us to pray in advance that the test will never be too hard for us to pass successfully.

Christ in Us, the Hope of Glory

In summary, imagine that we can observe simultaneously all that is going on in earth and heaven. On earth, some of God's people realize the need to pray. Perhaps they are desperate for some kind of material provision. Maybe they are driven to their knees by grief over sin and failure. Or they find themselves struggling for the right against seemingly insurmountable odds. Whatever the precise circumstances, they turn to God.

But now let us turn the spotlight on heaven. What do we find? God is using those very providences of the life and times of His people to shape them into the image of His beloved Son. At the same time, the Holy Spirit is taking deeper possession of their hearts, so that He is able to reecho the intercessions of their risen Head within them.

For example, Judy was quite unaware that this is exactly what the Holy Spirit was doing in her prayers. Think how much more logical it was to pray for healing, which is what her husband did! Yet it never crossed her mind. Why?

God had a special blessing for her, which she could never have sought on her own. Jesus' desire was for her deeper spiritual maturity, and the Holy Spirit echoed this prayer in her.

Through all the hard times and the pleas for help, the most wonderful thing in all the world is happening, the very thing for which God created this universe: the lineaments of the character of Jesus are being worked into His people and the voice of Jesus Himself is breaking through their prayers. What is more, the Father on His throne is hearing it.

But that is not all. The world is being changed and His namc is being hallowed, as He grants provision, pardon, and protection in answer to the cries of those who abide in His Son.

All of us value the kind of maturity that makes us productive and valuable members of society. But we must never forget the potential influence that *spiritual* maturity can have. Believing, persistent prayer can radically affect both our own development as Christians and society as a whole. The life of John Knox offers us public testimony to that truth. Yet, the final measure of maturity is not the public recognition, but the likeness to Christ. When we begin to take seriously the truth that prayer changes us, surely it should provide us with the strongest motivation to take prayer more seriously.

May God grant us such maturity and power in prayer!

So I sought for
a man among them
who would make a wall,
and stand in the gap
before Me
on behalf of the land,
that I should not destroy it;
but I found no one.
(Ezekiel 22:30)

5

PRAYER
CHANGES OTHERS

S ince we have now reached the place where we are
ready to focus on how prayer influences others, it
may be the place to find out the other half of the story of
the young student who prayed for two years! What was
going on in the life of the girl as a result?

Shortly after he made up his mind to take the matter to
the Lord, she had a heated argument with her roommate
one evening. At the time she was in preparation for missionary service (she thought) and her friend was rebuking
her for showing no interest in marriage.

A Hidden Influence!

She began to wonder if the Lord had other plans when she
opened her Bible that night and turned to the place that
she had reached in the book of Psalms in the course of her
regular daily reading. The last verses of the psalm came as
a shock: "He maketh the barren woman to keep house, and
to be a joyful mother of children" (Psalm 113:9, KJV).

Somehow, although she was not very good at hearing the Lord's voice, this time she knew He had spoken!

However, she was quite sure that it could not have anything to do with the American that she had come to know and respect. For one thing, how on earth could he be interested in her, since she had so very much to learn in the Christian life? And for another, he seemed to have absolutely no call to the mission field.

She did notice that they got along extremely well, and they often ended up together after class and at student and church activities, so that they became close friends. His strong Christian background contrasted with her rather more humanist one, so she was delighted whenever she could ask him for help in integrating her faith and studies. He encouraged her to begin reading through the Bible in a year, which was something she had never considered.

So she began to grow in the faith, all the while with her eyes set on South America — not North America! And she dated several other people briefly, but always felt under a constraint that they were not in the will of God for her.

Finally, in her senior year, she went to a conference organized by a missionary society with special interest in South America. She expected that she would see "green lights" flashing and begin the application process. But that did not happen. She came home absolutely sure that she had been mistaken about being called to the mission field.

Only then was she finally free to admit to herself that she had actually fallen in love with the American! She wrestled in prayer until about two in the morning, when a second time, she felt that Psalm 113 had indeed been spoken directly to her and knew that the Lord was giving her the go-ahead in the relationship.

Next morning, when the boy saw her, he asked her about the conference. She told him that she would not be going to the mission field after all, but said no more! That, of course, was his cue.

The Results of Intercession

His prayer had changed her. Those two years had given her time to develop some Christian maturity. She had learned a great deal about Christian things and had seen God changing her actions and attitudes.

Had he spoken earlier, she would not have been ready at all. She might have refused, or at the very least, been much less well equipped to be the kind of wife he needed. By praying rather than speaking, he did the best thing for them both.

Now this example reflects the influence of prayer in the life of just one other person, on a small scale and without particularly far-reaching consequences. But think what could happen if God's people as a whole, as a church as well as individually, would look to Him for changes on earth. Can we have the confidence that it would hold true on a wider level that prayer changes others? What do the Scriptures really teach?

So far in our examination of the second, or manward, half of the Lord's Prayer, we have discussed the corporate needs and destiny of the people of God, and in particular have focused on what God is doing *in* His people. Now we will consider what God is doing *through* His people. This brings us to the great subject of intercession — praying for others in order that God's name may be hallowed, His kingdom come, and His will done.

We have already noticed that the thrust of the second part of the Lord's Prayer is corporate: we pray not only for our own "daily bread," though that is of course right, but Christ expects us to get outside ourselves and remember others. So what exactly does it mean to be an intercessor?

Remembering that the Lord's Prayer is in many ways a magnet for all that the rest of Scripture has to say on the topic, it will help us to look in some detail at two episodes in the life of ancient Israel. Both offer convincing evidence that the work of the kingdom of God really is determined so powerfully by whether or not there is intercession.

Moses' Prayer Saved the Day

Psalm 106 gives a summary of the history of Israel. It lists God's gracious dealings with His people. Yet after all His mercies, "They forgot God their Savior, who had done great things in Egypt, wondrous works in the land of Ham, awesome things by the Red Sea. Therefore He said that He would destroy them" (vv. 21–23). Why did He not do so?

Notice carefully the sole factor which preserved them: God's judgment would have fallen, "had not Moses His chosen one *stood before Him in the breach*, to turn away His wrath" from His erring people (v. 23, emphasis added). This actual event is recorded in Exodus 32, and you will no doubt remember the story of how Moses interceded. According to Psalm 106:23, it was this intercession alone which spared an entire nation from utter destruction.

Do you remember the children's story of the little Dutch boy who saved his village from destruction? On his way home one evening, he noticed a trickle of water seeping through the dike, or sea wall, that protected the surrounding countryside from the North Sea.

Now, Holland is a land that is largely below sea-level. Much of the country has been reclaimed from the sea and is sheltered by huge dikes painstakingly built over the years. The safety of the population depends upon the maintenance of these walls.

The little boy knew at once that the smallest breach could mean disaster and death. He knew that if he even took the time to go for help, the sea would have an opportunity to enlarge the hole and force its way through in a flood. So he put his finger in the gap and faithfully held it there.

Late that night, a search party sent out by his anxious mother found him fast asleep, with his whole arm thrust into the dike. Aware of the danger, his prompt and selfless action probably saved the lives of many.

An intercessor is like that, protecting others from the times when "the enemy comes in like a flood," by asking that the "Spirit of the Lord will lift up a standard against him" (Isaiah 59:19).

No One to Stand in the Gap

In the prophecy of Ezekiel 22, there is a situation which is the precise opposite of Psalm 106:23. In Moses' time, the people were spared and went on to live through the period of greatest blessing in their history, all because of the intercession of one man. Now notice the contrast in Ezekiel where the people of Israel again have grievously sinned, and God's wrath has gone out against them.

On this occasion, there is not a Moses who is able to
stand in the gap and intercede for them. "So I sought for a
man among them who would make a wall, and stand in
the gap before Me on behalf of the land, that I should not
destroy it; but I found no one" (v. 30). To state it simply,
when there was no intercessor to stand in the gap, it was
all over for Israel.

Maybe, living at a time of constant threat of military
invasion of his beloved Israel, Ezekiel had in mind the picture of a city under siege, where the enemy has just succeeded in opening up a breach in the defenses. He seems
to be likening the need for an intercessor to the need for
even one soldier who would offer his life as a shield
against the adversary preparing to rush in on the helpless
townspeople inside.

Now Israel's lack of an intercessor in this later stage of
its history must, of course, be understood in light of its
continual violations of God's covenant. The fact that they
had turned their back on God so many different times was
one of the reasons why there was nobody there to stand in
the gap and intercede for them.

The divine logic is simple and sobering: when there
was a "Moses," when there was somebody who interceded, destruction was averted. Revival ultimately came.
But when they reached a time when there was no one interceding, destruction came instead. Israel had to suffer
seventy years of exile and slavery in pagan Babylon.

Jesus the Great Intercessor

Now let us move briefly to the New Testament and to *the*
intercessor. The previous chapter reminded us of the impor-

tance of remembering our union with the Lord Jesus
Christ. We must not forget Him here either. The only way
we will not become "burned out" and discouraged in this
very hard work of intercession is to draw on what we are
in Him.

All believers who read these lines are undoubtedly
fighting a battle to get themselves in line with the purposes
of God for their lives. That means that some of us are
going to have to rearrange some priorities and make some
changes, if we are to hear what God is saying to us here.

We can only make these fruitful changes under the condition that we continually keep our eyes on Jesus, remembering that we are doing this work in unity with Him. So
before I lay any further responsibility on you for intercession, I must first lift up Jesus, the greatest intercessor of all.

Before He went out to the Garden of Gethsemane, on
up to Pilate's hall, and then to Calvary, Jesus prayed what
has come to be known as the great "high priestly prayer"
of John 17, where He said, "For their sakes I sanctify my-
self, that they also may be sanctified by the truth," (v.19.)
This prayer, as well as everything that Jesus did in His
life, suffering, and death was for his people. The Cross
was simply the culmination of it all.

There we see Him, not just on his knees, but literally
"standing in the gap" bodily, in order to take on Himself
the wrath of God which otherwise ought to destroy us.
Here indeed is one greater than Moses, not only interceding with God for others, but taking God's wrath upon
Himself, exhausting its punishment in Himself.

Thus He makes it possible for us to be brought back to
the Father and find incredible mercy, love, and healing—
not tremendous wrath coming out against us—all because

of the one who stood in the gap between our sinful souls
and a perfectly holy God.

"He Lives Forever Making Intercession"

As Paul says, Jesus "was delivered up because of our of-
fenses, and was raised because of our justification" (Romans 4:25). His glorified body has been taken out of the
realm of our physical sight. Yet He still has His body; it is
just as real as when He was on the earth. So what is He
doing now? The letter to the Hebrews teaches that in a real
sense His whole ministry has now become one of prayer.

While there is much we do not know about the activities of Christ in the heavenly realm, Hebrews does teach
that the focus of the ministry of our risen Lord is as our
High Priest, continually engaged in intercession for His
people. He is still in the gap! Do you know why those of
us who belong to Him will not be destroyed? Because
there is somebody in the gap for us.

The Lord Jesus Christ is there at the throne of God on
our behalf, even while you are reading these words! Thus
if you feel that your prayers are worthless, you should not
despair. Indeed, none of us should ever feel that we may
just as well give up praying, for somebody is in the gap
for you and me.

This means that it is actually possible for us to wield
enormous power in prayer by getting down into the gap
with Him. There we can reflect His intercession and make
lasting changes in this world. We can be instrumental in
averting the wrath of God, rolling back the wickedness of
the devil, and bringing down beauty, love, goodness, truth,
and salvation.

Of course, we can intercede only because He is already interceding for us. Hear Hebrews 4:14–16 and 7:24–25:

Seeing then that we have a great High Priest who has passed through the heavens, Jesus the Son of God, let us hold fast our confession. For we do not have a High Priest who cannot sympathize with our weaknesses, but was in all points tempted as we are, yet without sin. Let us therefore come boldly to the throne of grace, that we may obtain mercy and find grace to help in time of need.

But He, because He continues forever, has an unchangeable priesthood. Therefore He is also able to save to the uttermost those who come to God through Him, since He ever lives to make intercession for them.

He Himself is on the throne, interceding for us! When we intercede, we reflect His own intercession. When we go into the gap for others, we actually meet His invisible presence there, and so we never intercede alone, but rather in union with Him.

Furthermore, as we look to Him, He will bring the help and the grace and the mercy that we need. Then gradually, He will fulfill His purposes in our lives and change us into His intercessors.

As we catch a fresh vision of how He is both praying *for* us as well as praying *in* us with His Spirit, we are motivated to do what we can to bring our lives in line with His purposes and begin to stand in the gap for other people. There will be a multitude of situations in which we will start bringing others to Him in prayer, asking Him to give one their daily bread, to forgive the sins of another, or keep a third out of a particular temptation, compromise, or disaster.

Our interceding like this, in union with our High Priest and thus reflecting His intercessions, makes all the difference in the way in which God controls the world. It is all part of His plan that our intercession for others should enable them to receive the bread, the pardon, and the protection.

A Divine, Detached Clock Maker?

One of our greatest problems today is an attitude that has almost sapped the life out of the churches. It has come to us from a philosophy known as deism, which became popular during the eighteenth-century French Enlightenment. Its proponents held that although there probably was a God, He was actually far removed from this world and did not interact with it by performing miracles, inspiring Scripture, regenerating lost souls, or answering prayer.

This god of the deists made the world like a clock, wound it up, and then left it to run down on its own. Thus the world was viewed as a closed mechanistic system into which God could not intervene.

It was therefore out of the question to imagine that prayer could really change anything in this real world. Deism held that, at best, prayer might help one to feel better psychologically, but on no account was the clock going to be sped up, slowed down, repaired, or changed as a result!

This view is now very much entrenched in the general worldview of Europe. In fact, a friend who grew up in England has often remarked that when she was studying history in high school, she could not begin to imagine a God who had anything to do with what happened in the world. He seemed totally outside it all. She was amazed to come to the southern part of the United States and discover that even people who did not profess conversion had no doubt at all that God is in fact in control, and could even point to instances where they felt He had intervened.

Practical Atheism

However, though we all know that the philosophy of deism is wrong according to the Word of God, I wonder if it is not really the way we so often think when it comes to actually *requesting* God to intervene? Do we not think like deists when it comes to prayer? The worldview so prevalent outside the church may after all have influenced many of us more than we know.

In a sense, we could identify the sin of the Eastern world as saying that God is the same thing as the whole world, thus ending up without a transcendent God at all. Oriental religion in its many forms, some of which have now been incorporated into the New Age movement, is essentially pantheistic: God is everything and everything is God.

Ultimately, the material world is considered simply part of an infinite, supreme Spirit, with no real distinction between God and man. But this makes God and nature identical, so that there is really no God, but only man claiming to be God!

On the other hand, the sin of the Western world is deism. Yes, there is a God, but He is totally outside the world. Natural law, or perhaps evolution, are often used as substitutes for the personal God of the Bible, in order to exclude Him from any serious interaction with the real world. In fact, Western society ends up as godless and as prayerless as the East! Is that an exaggeration?

If we really believed that God was intervening in this world all the time, in answer to the prayers of His people, and if we were convinced that it is our prayers that change the course of lives as well as nations, would not hundreds of thousands of believers be giving top priority to standing in the gap and interceding? Would not the church in our Western cultures be praying a great deal more? Surely we have become deists in practice, if not in name!

So we need to leave the cold, empty world of deism, and go to the real world of God's truth, which is neither empty nor silent. The Bible tells us what the world is really like and provides us with the inside story on how everything really works.

Remember that the Bible is the truth of God, and say to yourself as you read a passage, "This is how things really are." If we say that and believe it, then we will be shifting ourselves over onto praying ground and out of dead deism! For the Western world to survive, somehow we must be set free from this deadening influence which has so successfully destroyed our commitment to gathering together for serious corporate prayer.

Aaron and Hur

Exodus 17:8–13 gives a wonderful illustration of the way God uses prayer to do amazing things in history. God's people were forced into battle with the Amalekites in which they were greatly outnumbered. Moses told Joshua to choose men and go out to fight the enemy. But he also said that he would stand on the top of the hill with the rod of God in his hand and pray.

As long as Moses held up his hands in prayer, then the people of God prevailed in the battle down in the valley. But like all of us, Moses was a man, and so his arms became heavier and heavier until his hands felt like lead weights! However, if he let his hands down from this position of intercession, then God's people began to lose to the pagans. So someone found a large rock and put it under him as a seat, and Aaron and Hur, the priests, supported his arms, one standing on either side of him. What happened? Because those two were helping Moses hold up his hands in intercession, God's people gloriously prevailed. Prayer was the deciding factor.

I know that is quite different from what most people think today in our deistic culture! We want to say that those kinds of things are just encouraging stories! But we will have to seriously adjust our thinking to the picture of the world given in God's Word, if we are going to get onto praying ground.

After all, the one who gave us the Scriptures is none other than *the* Truth. He is light and in Him there is no darkness at all, nor the least deception. He is the one who says that we can believe what Exodus 17 teaches about intercession being the deciding factor in winning battles.

Superhuman Resources

Today, just as in Old Testament times, human resources are not enough. If we are going to win the battles, for example, against secularism, humanism, and the occult, and against evil things in our own lives, we have got to hold up one another's hands in intercession. Often it is tiresome to intercede. It wears us out and wears us down, but we must do it to win the battle and turn the tide. God is saying that to His church.

In fact, these kinds of battles are going on and, more importantly, being won all over the place. In most cases no one ever knows about them, except those who are personally involved. But there is no doubt that when history is finally written we will be amazed at where it has taken a different turn for no other reason than that the Lord's people took Him at His word and began to pray.

A group of Christian women were involved in a local Right to Life Chapter in a small town in northern California. Among other things, they shared a concern for the general moral tone of the community, so when they heard that a bar in town was planning to introduce a striptease act as part of the entertainment, they were most disturbed.

Their first reaction was to besiege City Hall with phone calls. But then someone remembered hearing a campaign plan drawn up by an organization called Christian Family Renewal that had been effective elsewhere in the country. The plan was called "Prayer and Action" and listed ten steps to be followed.

The first was to contact area churches and ask them to pray simply for God's will to be done. That way as many churches as possible would be involved. Then it listed the various levels of city and county government that might need to be contacted. As a start, these different local authorities were to be prayed for regularly. The final steps would be to actually seek to influence the legislative processes.

So they called as many churches as they could, and they started to pray themselves. They also began to gather "ammunition" from other sources in case they had to go to the city council with a proposal for a new ordinance, not really knowing what to expect.

But it was all unnecessary. They never needed to proceed to the action part of the plan. As far as they knew, no one had ever actually complained directly to the management. Yet with no fanfare, the bar owner simply sold out one day and left town, and the buyer was not interested in continuing the entertainment. A quiet, but nevertheless significant victory had been won by prayer alone. Like Moses, they had stood in the gap.

Overflowing Prayer Meetings!

If the church as a whole really starts believing what Exodus 17 — and many other passages — teach about prayer, then the prayer meetings in the evangelical churches all over the world will fill to overflowing every week! They will no longer be held in a small downstairs hall but up in the main sanctuary.

Indeed, if we really took seriously what God's Word says about the power of prayer, our churches could not accommodate those who would come to pray! We would have to rent warehouses, football stadiums, and perhaps put up huge tents, just as they did in Scotland, Northern Ireland, and the southern United States during the days and weeks of prayer connected with the 1858–1859 revival.

If we really believed the explanation given for the victory of Moses' army, our church officials would have difficulty trying to find tents large enough to hold the people who would be crowding in to pray! That may happen yet, and it probably will. But how many churches do we know at present that have a seating problem on Wednesday night?

A Spiritual Battle

The hour for our culture is late, and so it is absolutely essential for us to understand that all the great battles presently going on in modern society are rooted in spiritual causes. Of course we are right to look carefully at the externals. We can certainly say that a particular problem is caused by, for example, political totalitarianism or the drug traffic or pornography or AIDS.

Any one of these explanations may well be true. These are indeed genuine problems in our world. The devil, undoubtedly, uses all kinds of things. But ultimately there is something manipulating all those other factors that we must recognize if we are going to make any lasting impact on our deep cultural crisis.

Even the little factors which hinder our lives from shining for Christ are often motivated by unseen spiritual powers. We must stop thinking like deists who assume there is only a material explanation for everything and that all we need to do is to look at material causes.

Now certainly, the material is both valid and important. As Christians we must always honor legitimate science and physical research as a way of serving the God who made all things. Yet at the same time, we understand that there is an absolutely real and immeasurably powerful *spiritual* realm behind this material world that is constantly impinging upon material reality.

This spiritual realm influences this world in both good and evil ways. This is where the Biblical theology of prayer comes in. Because of their union with His Son, God gives His saints authority to turn the tide and thus win these spiritual battles which affect our material world. Only intercessory prayer by the church can win the day. That is the way reality worked in the time of Moses and of Paul, and that is how it is today. So when will we, as whole congregations, return to prayer?

Of course, the Christian church has to do more than pray. We are commanded to preach, to administer the sacraments, to evangelize, and to live holy lives of love, ser-

vice, and compassion to a needy world. We are to glorify
God in our personal professions and in our societal institutions.

Scripture teaches a beautiful balance between prayer
and action. And yet I detect a tendency among believers of
both liberal and conservative persuasions to neglect prayer
in favor of action. Only intercessory prayer, only massive
prayer, can make all our human action effective to win this
battle.

Two illustrations of the power of intercession will encourage us to join others in this mightiest of all battles,
now going on "in the gap" between the seen and the unseen worlds.

"The Spirit Comes in Answer to Prayer"

In 1858, the largest Presbyterian church in the Carolinas,
and probably in the entire southern United States, was
Zion Church in Charleston, South Carolina. It had a white
pastor, John L. Girardeau, who was a Southern Presbyterian, but it was a black church. There was a regular Sunday attendance of over fifteen hundred black people. Some
of them were free but most were slaves. There were also
about three hundred white people regularly attending. Un-
like most Southerners of his day, Girardeau insisted that
the blacks be given the best seats and the whites be put in
the galleries.

The members of this church felt the need of revival
and began to pray for it earnestly in 1858. In the late
1850s, there was a growing spiritual movement that
stretched up and down the east coast of North America
and then swept across to Great Britain resulting in the
1859 revival. In 1858, Girardeau and the faithful black

members of this unusual and vital church wanted the Holy
Spirit for themselves and for Charleston.

Listen to a description of how their prayers for the
Spirit were answered from Girardeau's biography (written
by his son-in-law, George A. Blackburn, who was present
when it happened):

> This began with a prayer meeting that constantly in-
> creased until the house was filled. Some of the officers
> of the church wanted him to commence preaching ser-
> vices, but he steadily refused, waiting for the outpouring
> of the Spirit.

> His view was that the Father had given to Jesus, as the
> King and Head of the church, the gift of the Holy Spirit,
> and that Jesus in His sovereign administration of the af-
> fairs of his church, bestowed him upon whomsoever He
> pleased, and in whatever measure He pleased. Day after
> day he, therefore, kept his prayer addressed directly to
> the mediatorial throne for the Holy Spirit in mighty re-
> viving power.

> One evening, while leading the people in prayer, he re-
> ceived a sensation as if a bolt of electricity had struck
> his head and diffused itself through his whole body. For
> a little while he stood speechless under the strange
> physical feeling. Then he said: "The Holy Spirit has
> come; we will begin preaching tomorrow evening."

> He closed the service with a hymn, dismissed the con-
> gregation, and came down from the pulpit; but no one
> left the house. The whole congregation had quietly re-
> sumed its seat. Instantly he realized the situation. The
> Holy Spirit had not only come to him — he had also
> taken possession of the hearts of the people.

> Immediately he began exhorting them to accept the
> Gospel. They began to sob, softly, like the falling of

rain; then, with deeper emotion, to weep bitterly or to rejoice loudly, according to their circumstances. It was midnight before he could dismiss his congregation.

The meeting went on night and day for eight weeks. Large numbers of both white and black were converted and joined the various churches of the city. His own was wonderfully built up, not only in numbers, but also in an experience that remained in the church.

He was accustomed to say that he could always count on those who were converted in that meeting. This was probably due to the deep work of conviction of sin, the protracted period of the conviction, the clear sense of pardon, and the joyful witness of the Spirit to their adoption.[1]

In the end, things worked out wonderfully to the glory of God as well as to the comfort of God's people in Charleston and far beyond. All this proves, beyond any shadow of a doubt, the truth of S. D. Gordon's observation: "Prayer is striking the winning blow; service is merely gathering up the results."[2] Or otherwise stated, you win your battles the night before in the prayer closet.

That is why the people of Zion Church prayed for the Spirit. While they knew that it was in the hands of God alone to give the Spirit, they also understood that intercession could be used to bring Him down, as God so willed. They interceded and God gloriously intervened.

Now a prayer for revival may not at first appear to be something that will change history. However, do you remember the words of Jesus to Paul on the road to Damascus? Paul's mission was to "open [the eyes of the Gentiles] and to turn them from darkness to light, and from the power of Satan to God" (Acts 26:18).

Imagine the potential impact on society when large
numbers of the population are no longer under the power
of the prince of this world, the prince of darkness. When a
believer's allegiance is changed on the inside, his actions
in society are different. When he is indwelt by the Holy
Spirit, he is no longer a "slave to sin."

The church then is in the position to be the preserving
agent for society, retarding moral decay, just as salt keeps
food from spoiling. In fact this is just what happened in
Charleston. Later on in the biography, George Blackburn
reveals an extraordinary secret of the War Between the
States:

Charleston was the citadel of the secession, and as such,
detested by the Federal authorities and most of the people of the North. Not a few of these yearned to see it
laid in ashes. . . . Several times efforts were made to secretly organize the negroes and through them start fires
at the same time in many parts of the city. Special
agents were employed to carry out such designs, and
more than once they almost succeeded.

After the war it became an open secret why these well-
laid schemes were frustrated. Some leaders of the negroes religiously believed that Dr. Girardeau was the
special representative of God to their race; and his
church a holy temple in which the Almighty delighted to
dwell.

They feared, and they imparted this fear to other leaders, that if negroes burned that city so dear to this man
of God, and that church so beloved and honored by the
Lord of heaven, *then* the divine curse might rest upon
them and heaven withhold that freedom, which they felt
was almost within their grasp.[3]

If you ever visit this charming historic city, which contains some of the architectural treasures of the Colonial South, take time to thank the Lord for using prayer, offered first for revival, to subsequently protect and preserve an entire community beyond the church doors! The conversions of some of those living in a neighborhood can indeed be a channel that brings to bear the influence of the blessing of God.

Since anyone who is abiding in Christ has special access to Him in prayer, we must take seriously the awesome privilege and responsibility of pleading the promises of Scripture before Him. The strongest prayer promise of all must surely be Romans 8:32: "He who did not spare His own Son, but delivered Him up for us all, how shall He not with Him also freely give us all things?" This means that the life and death of His own Son for sinners provides us with the primary evidence that God is committed to intervening in history. If the cross of Jesus brought about the defeat of the devil, then surely nothing else on this earth is beyond divine power. That assurance should encourage us to pray if nothing else will.

The Outer Isles of Scotland

Although the culture and circumstances were markedly different, the spiritual dynamics were much the same in the revival that occurred in the late 1940s and early 1950s on the Isle of Lewis, off the northwest coast of Scotland.

In that remote highland Gaelic culture, two elderly ladies (one of them bent double with arthritis) became burdened about the worldliness and spiritual deadness of the youth on their island. For three or four years, three times a day, these humble Christians in their little white stone cottage overlooking the stormy North Atlantic, urgently be-

sought God to send down His Holy Spirit with convicting
and converting power on their community.

According to the writings of the late Rev. Duncan
Campbell, who was greatly used in the revival, the Holy
Spirit suddenly came down one Saturday night on a large
group of formerly worldly minded young people assembled
in a dance hall behind a pub! Many of them were broken
down and regenerated by the power of God on the spot.

The movement spread throughout many parts of the island and savingly touched large numbers of people over
the next few years. Once again, someone (in this case two
elderly ladies) had stood in the gap and had brought down
the mercy of God upon an entire community, with results
that last to this day. In fact, travelers who visit the Islands
are struck by the peace and tranquility and the gentle grace
of the islanders. Yet in most cases they are completely unaware that what they are experiencing is the result of the
work of the Holy Spirit.

A Challenge to Every Congregation

Two things are certain: in the model prayer, Christ has
called us to pray for one another to be given provision,
pardon, and protection. In addition we have these—and
many other—glorious examples of God's glad willingness
to pour out His Spirit when His saints intercede.

At the time of the Second Great Awakening, when revival swept through America, it became common to see
benches set out across the front of the churches, where peni-
tent members of the congregation and those seeking salvation would come to kneel and pray as the Holy Spirit im-
pressed upon them their need for forgiveness and renewal.

Most of our churches these days do not have "mourners' benches" across the front. If they did, entire congregations should fill them, from one side to another, falling to their knees together and seeking God's forgiveness for not praying. Of course we realize that "mourners' benches," prayer rooms, and confessional meetings, or even bended knees and weeping eyes, are not so much the point, as is the need for hearts genuinely repentant over lack of prayer.

Must we not ask God to forgive us for being practical deists? Should we not ask God to forgive us for doubting His word; for not asking His Holy Spirit to be poured out upon us to change us; for being too stingy to give Him five minutes in the day? Should we not ask God to forgive our elders, bishops, deacons, and Sunday school teachers for not organizing prayer meetings as a major church activity? But then we should move on to take a positive and constructive course of action.

Much as we church people need to mourn for our sin of deistic-type prayerlessness, at the same time we need to do something specific in hopes of remedying the situation. If all that we have said is true, what is more desperately needed at this hour than corporate church prayer meetings? Remember: *our* bread; *our* debts; lead *us* not into temptation, but deliver *us* from evil.

Should not the goal of any church be to have as many people in a weekly prayer meeting as it does on a Sunday morning? Prayer is no less important than preaching and worship! Why should just a few members carry the load for everyone? Surely that same congregation that fills the church at 11 A.M. on Sunday morning ought to be there at, for example, 7:30 on Wednesday night.

Of course, the day of the week and the particular hour do not matter — that depends entirely on local conditions.

But the principle of a weekly prayer meeting of the *entire* congregation is absolutely vital to the work of God in your community.

The Power of a Congregational Prayer Meeting

Cell groups (good as they are) cannot replace the corporate, congregational prayer meeting. Men's prayer groups, singles, or college, or young mothers' prayer meetings are excellent. All of these have their place. After all, look at the effects of the prayers of two ladies in Scotland!

However, it is a serious mistake to let any special group replace the congregational prayer meeting. Any evangelical congregation ought to know and be constantly reminded that its central work is preaching the Word, praying that Word out into the pews and into the world, and exhibiting a caring, Christ-like fellowship in their daily lives toward one another and the world.

Preaching, fellowship, even meeting the needs of the community and individuals with compassionate deeds of service (all of which are essential to a living church of Christ) will not be sufficient to win the spiritual battles of this generation without congregational prayer.

That kind of prayer during the week anoints the minister's Sabbath words and sets them on fire with the Spirit. It binds Satan, combating his influence on the church body as a whole and in individuals, in a way that does not take place without a mutual agreement and binding in the all-prevailing name of Jesus. In addition, a congregational prayer meeting builds a committed fellowship of prayer warriors who will stand for Christ and His Word in that local situation against all intruders.

To do the work of God, churches simply must do more than preach on Sunday morning. If there is no prayer meeting during the week, then the most painstakingly prepared and eloquently delivered sermon can only have half the potential impact, if as much as that. Is it a coincidence that the world's largest churches — such as Yoido Full Gospel, with half a million members, and two or three major Presbyterian churches of fifty thousand each, not to mention several others with over ten thousand members — are in Seoul, Korea, where the tradition of large all-night and early morning prayer meetings is so strong? The lack of commitment to prayer on the part of the congregations is why churches remain feeble and so many pastors have broken hearts. A pastor simply cannot carry the spiritual load on his own.

We need to realize that the congregational prayer meeting has a unique authority from God to bring down unction upon the minister and impel his preaching from the pulpit out into the pews. He needs the fire of heaven brought down first upon his words and then upon the lives of those who hear.

Cosmic Proportions

The prayer meeting, furthermore, has authority from God to bring protection over the moral life of its Christian leaders. How greatly this moral protection is needed in church and Christian agencies today! All across the world we hear of famous Christian leaders who lose their whole ministries and bring reproach on the Christian cause for having succumbed to sexual temptations. This is obviously one of the major points at which Satan is currently attacking the church. How encouraging to know that faithful church prayer meetings have divine authority to rebuke Satan in prayer, in accordance with the Master's instructions, "lead us not into temptation."[4]

As much as every local church needs the protection and power that only a congregational prayer meeting can give it, no Biblically balanced group of intercessors will ever be content to concentrate merely upon their own particular ecclesiastical concerns—legitimate as these are. Those who pray the most regularly open themselves to the Spirit-engendered burden for the needs of the world and life of the nations. And the Bible makes no secret of how utterly dependent the crisis-ridden world is upon the intercessions of the people of God.

Incredible and ludicrous though it may be to the strictly secularist mind, the Biblical teaching on prayer clearly reveals the immense power and influence wielded by praying believers over world affairs. Simply stated, without public notice or popular approbation, congregational prayer meetings have a major hand in shaping the development of political and economic affairs. Occasionally, they even determine the outcome of military battles and international conflicts.

While little is known about the overall impact of the student demonstrations for freedom in China's Tiananman Square during the summer of 1989, apparently some of the leadership was Christian. Certainly, some fellowships came under increased surveillance as the demonstrations progressed. Though it is only conjecture, it seems eminently reasonable to suppose that, with as many Christians as there now apparently are in that great country, many must be praying against the repression of the gospel. Could the movement for freedom, there and in other communist countries, be related to intercession by the Lord's people, inside and outside borders?

Prayer Strikes the Winning Blow

The tenth chapter of the prophecy of Daniel shows that at the end of the Babylonian captivity of Israel, Daniel realized, through reading the prophecy of Jeremiah, that the seventy years of foreign bondage were nearly over. These seventy years, which were required to purge the people of God from their idolatry, were soon to be ended so that the captives could joyfully return to the land of their fathers.

Now Daniel was wise enough to know that the blessings that God had promised would have to be prayed down. Too often the people of God fail to understand and can forget that the blessings of God in His promises have to be prayed into execution. But Daniel knew it; Girardeau of Charleston knew it; and those ladies on the Isle of Lewis knew it, too.

So Daniel began interceding for God to bless His people so they could go home. He confessed sin, cried out for mercy on the basis of scriptural promises, and thus "stood in the gap." He was told later that from the time he began to pray, a great struggle went on in the heavenlies for the life of that nation. The devil was angry and resisting divine influence. Both good and evil angels were involved in this titanic, unseen battle. Which way would it go?

Eventually Daniel's continuing prayer turned the tide of the battle by bringing in another powerful angel who tipped the balances and thus overcame the evil one and his forces. We are clearly told that it was only through the intercession of Daniel that the second angel was brought in. The prayers of that one man changed the course of the history of the people of Israel, brought them back to their homeland, and unleashed upon them the blessings of God for generations to come.

The Supreme Weapon

Do we not realize that in the same way there is a struggle for the soul of our own country and the other nations of the world today? Are we not aware that behind events that look so seemingly innocent, there are dark malign powers doing battle to get the souls of our children as well as our own souls. The devil is actively trying to stop us as a missionary force and to destroy any Christian influence in the various cultures thoughout the world.

The only way that this battle is going to be won is for God's church to repent of its prayerlessness, its unbelief, and its lack of faith in Him. We have no choice but to go down together to our knees, praying for one another, pleading the blood of Jesus, so that whatever needs to be done in the spiritual realm will be done.

This is what it will take for victory to be given to Christ's church. We must intercede until Christ, in the words of Isaiah 53:11, "shall see the travail of His soul, and be satisfied," as millions are won to Him throughout the world.

Intercession must once again become the vital center of the church's life if we are to move the nations Godward and please the heart of Him who taught His church to pray: "Give us this day our daily bread. And forgive us our debts as we forgive our debtors. And lead us not into temptation, but deliver us from the evil one."[5]

Once the church—in the steps of its divine master—makes intercession for others its top priority, there will be profound results. Not only will a lost world be blessed, but its members will know, in their daily experience, the reality described by the nineteenth-century Anglican scholar, Dr. Trench:

> We kneel and all about us seems to lower;
> We rise and all the distant and the near
> Stands forth in sunny outline, brave and clear
> We kneel, how weak!
> We rise, how full of power.[6]

PART 3

OUR PROBLEMS AND GOD'S SOLUTIONS

Because of his persistence
he will rise
and give him as many
as he needs.
(Luke 11:8)

6

THE CHALLENGE TO PERSEVERE

S ome of you may be familiar with the story of the Danish noblewoman, Baroness Blixen, which was popularized recently in the movie *Out of Africa*. She lived in Kenya and was the owner of a huge coffee plantation. On part of this plantation there also lived some of the Kikuyu tribe, whom she grew to love. But because of financial reverses after the First World War, she lost the land including the property on which these Kikuyu lived.

Unfortunately the new owners were planning to put the tribal people off the land where they had lived from time immemorial. The baroness did everything she could to save it for them. Since she had lost her money she could not buy it and give it to them, but she tried to go through the various governmental channels to see if the homeland of these beloved people could be spared.

After having failed at every turn, the movie version of her story showed the distinguished, attractive baroness attending a large reception for the new governor of Kenya. She made her way through the crowds to join the receiving line of VIPs assembled in honor of the governor and his wife.

Then, out of sheer desperation, she disregarded proto-
col, and in front of these immaculately groomed socialites,
fell on her knees and grabbed the governor's hands, held
on to them, and started pleading for her Kikuyu! Shocked
guests tried to pull her up, but she continued to beg the
governor to give his word that he would look into the matter. Suddenly the governor's wife stood up and stated,
"You have mine!"

Why was she successful, against all the rules of decorum as well as governmental procedures? Immune to em-
barrassment because of the urgency of her need, that distinguished woman got down on her hands and knees in
public to plead with the governor himself. She was shameless. You could say that she was not easily embarrassed
because she loved so much.

This reconstruction of events parallels in many ways
the kind of attitude that will help us deal with discourage-
ments in prayer, because any realistic study of the theology of the subject must admit that some difficult problems
do exist. Whenever we commit ourselves to pray for the
salvation of the lost, the blessing of the church, or the
glory of God, discouraging obstacles often surface.

But the Christ who gave us the Lord's Prayer also
gave us the solutions to the major difficulties which face
anyone who begins seriously praying. In the version of the
prayer found in Luke 11, after the familiar words of the
"Our Father," Christ deals directly with what may well be
the greatest problem of them all.

Perseverance in Prayer

Jesus Himself, who was always heard by the Father, gives
us a form of prayer, and then with all the wisdom of God

that He had and was, He launches into a problem that prayer raises. He candidly acknowledges to us that problems exist. Some of the difficulties related to prayer could be reduced to the matter that He attacks head-on in Luke 11:5–13, not with a theory or commandments, but with a story:

> Which of you shall have a friend, and go to him at midnight and say unto him, "Friend, lend me three loaves; for a friend of mine has come to me on his journey, and I have nothing to set before him"; and he will answer from within and say, "Do not trouble me; the door is now shut, and my children are with me in bed; I cannot rise and give to you"?
>
> I say to you, though he will not rise and give to him because he is his friend, yet because of his persistence he will rise and give him as many as he needs.
>
> And I say to you, ask, and it will be given to you; seek, and you will find; knock, and it will be opened to you. For everyone who asks receives, and he who seeks finds, and to him who knocks it will be opened.
>
> If a son asks for bread from any father among you, will he give him a stone? Or if he asks for a fish, will he give him a serpent instead of a fish? Or if he asks for an egg, will he offer him a scorpion? If you then, being evil, know how to give good gifts to your children, how much more will your heavenly Father give the Holy Spirit to those who ask Him!

How does Jesus encourage us here? He wants us to learn that if our prayer is not answered positively the first time, we must *keep on asking* for our requests to prevail. Sometimes they will be answered immediately, but very often that will not be the case. When that happens, Jesus says for us to keep on asking, just like the baroness and this friend. God will be moved to answer our pleas and our crying by the very fact that we have kept on asking.

On the other hand, if there are occasions when we stop too soon, then we will not receive the blessing He really had in store for us. That is clearly the teaching of Jesus in this passage.

Never Be Ashamed to Keep On Asking

Notice in the text of Luke 11 the word *persistence*. You may be familiar with the old English word *importunity*, used in this context in the King James Version of the Bible. It could be translated into modern English equally well by the words *shamelessness*, *without shame*, *unabashed*, or *without being easily embarrassed*.

The man in the illustration was heard because he was shameless. He was not at all embarrassed to keep beating on the door and saying, "Please help me out. Someone has come to stay with me, and I've just got to have help." He ran the risk of looking like a fool in order to get the answer.

Similarly, the widow whose story is told in Luke was heard by the unjust judge because she kept pestering him. One translation of the Bible says that the judge heard the widow because she bothered him so much. Both were heard because of their shamelessness, which was actually commended by Jesus! It is hard to imagine God commending the kind of persistence that we normally despise in a salesman who refuses to take his foot out of our front door—but He does!

Part of the reason that we are so seldom heard as a church may be that we are too prim and proper! Perhaps the trouble is that we are bound by a false decorum which dictates that if we do not immediately get what we ask, we become too embarrassed to keep kneeling and crying out. Instead we simply let the matter drop.

When the devil comes to tempt us, he will whisper to us that it is foolish to be continually praying on and on and on. "It doesn't show good manners," he will say. "It's humiliating! I don't see other people doing it. If God wanted to give you what you think you need, He would have given it before now. After all, you've already prayed two whole months."

Then what do we do? We begin to agree! We find ourselves saying, "The thing for me to do is simply to quit. Perhaps I will pray for something else later on, but I will drop this unanswered request for now."

What kind of person will actually be enabled to pray down His glory into this world, hallow His name among men, advance His kingdom, and get His will done in their particular circumstances or in the wider community? Jesus tells us that it is someone who will be utterly shameless and completely unembarrassed, and thus keep on asking, just like the widow, or the Danish baroness, who was literally prepared to grovel in the dust.

Fifty-Three Years of Praying for a Friend

In fact, it is this kind of unabashed and almost brazen spirit, that will not be put off or be embarrassed, which will finally win the battle. When we approach the almighty throne with this sort of determination, then God's glory and salvation through Jesus Christ will sweep like a mighty tide through the nations. The secret is to keep on praying. Indeed, we need to increase our praying at the very time the world is saying that our persistence is shameful, foolish, or even fanatical!

An elderly lady from the western Highlands of Scotland, without knowing so, taught me a great deal about prayer. Though she had little formal education, she was deeply and beautifully schooled in the things of the Spirit. Many years ago I was in her home for a meal right after she had received a most encouraging letter.

A close friend of hers — another woman who was also in her eighties — wrote to say she had just come to a personal, saving knowledge of the grace of God in the Lord Jesus Christ. Perhaps unknown to her, my saintly friend had started to pray for the other's salvation soon after she had been a bridesmaid in her wedding. And she had been praying the same thing every day for the last fifty-three years! What perseverance!

Why the Wait?

Why is it that answers to specific requests, which seem to accord with the glory of God, are often delayed for so long? Why do we have to become so shameless to obtain the answer?

It seems as though we have a God who loves for us to become so desperate that at last we realize we have come to an end of ourselves and to an end of human resources. We have to discover that we simply cannot handle everything by ourselves; that all our cleverness, all our talents, all our family or business connections, and all our education are totally insufficient. Sometimes only that sort of situation can make us become desperate and determined enough to throw ourselves on His mercy and keep crying out. And it seems that our God is touched by that kind of desperation.

So why are answers to specific requests delayed for so long? Why do we have to persevere unabashed for weeks, months, and years with certain requests that God eventually does answer with a tremendous and happy yes? I am not speaking here of something that is outside God's will, or of something He finally denies, but of something that honors His name, something which eventually He does grant to the one who keeps on asking.

While the ultimate answer is hidden in the wisdom and goodness of God, nevertheless, we are given some insights from Scripture that may encourage us in hard circumstances.

Satanic Hindrances

One of the reasons why we have to keep on praying is that in some mysterious way, Satan resists our prayers. He is active in the unseen spiritual world, which actually has important and direct effects upon this world.

For example, we have already looked at Daniel 10 and seen how evil powers hindered the answer to his prayer for Israel. In fact an evil angel hindered the answer for three whole weeks but was unable to stop it completely. Why? It was Daniel's unembarrassed persistence that won through and added a factor in the unseen spiritual struggle. In an extraordinary way, the prayers of a man determined the victory in the spiritual conflict!

The angel Gabriel explained to Daniel in a vision that he only overcame when another angel was sent into the fray with him. If Daniel had given up after two weeks that help would not have come. Perseverance in believing prayer brought down the blessing. Who knows how long it will take to reverse the hold of the devil over Islamic and communist countries, and over others where God's people are dreadfully oppressed?

The point is this: Satan can hinder our prayers, but he cannot stop them being answered if we continue with perseverance. But if we let his hindrances discourage us so that we give up, then we may possibly lose a blessing that was in store for us or for someone for whom we were praying.

The message of Daniel 10, Luke 11, and Luke 18 is clear: if we persevere, the blessing will come. Our perseverance in prayer on earth has a hand in determining the battle raging in the unseen world because of satanic resistance. Thus the only way to be successful with hard prayer requests is to keep on praying. The way to be sure to lose is to quit!

"The Power of Believing Prayer Is Simply Irresistible"

Andrew Murray discusses the solution to the problem of unanswered prayer in his wonderful book, *With Christ in the School of Prayer.*[1] In a most helpful and practical way, he explains the story of the widow who had been wronged and the judge who would not give her justice. He helps us see why God delays answering His own elect and forces them to come to Him continually and shamelessly for help.

First, Murray points out that there are two contrasting statements in this parable. On the one hand, Christ says that God "bears long with [his elect]", yet on the other, "he will avenge them speedily." How do these two realities fit together? Christ says that God takes His time in answering His children, but in the very next breath, tells us that He takes swift action!

That is the tension which requires us to persevere in prayer. In other words, as we persevere in prayer, our God is doing two things in our lives. First, as it says of the widow and the unjust judge, He will be longsuffering, He will be "bearing long" over you — doing all kinds of things in your experience which require time. But secondly, and just as certainly, He is going "to avenge you speedily" as you persevere and ask in Jesus' name. What can this mean?

God Waits Until the Time Is Ripe

Murray draws the most heartening conclusion. He offers us the most powerful encouragement for perseverance because he is convinced that Jesus is assuring us that "the power of believing prayer is simply irresistible":

> Real faith can never be disappointed. It knows how, just as water, to exercise the irresistible power it can have, must be gathered up and accumulated, until the stream can come down in full force, there must often be a heaping up of prayer, until God sees that the measure is full, and the answer comes.

> It knows how, just as the ploughman has to take his ten thousand steps, and sow his ten thousand seeds, each one a part of the preparation for the final harvest, so there is a need-be for oft-repeated persevering prayer, all working out some desired blessing. It knows for certain that not a single believing prayer can fail of its effect in heaven, but has its influence, and is treasured up to work out an answer in due time to him who perseveres to the end.

He will avenge them speedily, the Master says. The blessing is all prepared; he is not only willing but most anxious to give them what they ask; everlasting love burns with the longing desire to reveal itself fully to its beloved, and to satisfy their needs.

God will not delay one moment longer than is absolutely necessary; He will do all in His power to hasten and speed the answer. He is long-suffering over them. "Behold! the husbandman waiteth for the precious fruit of the earth, being long suffering over it, till it receive the early and the latter rain." The husbandman does indeed long for his harvest, but knows that it must have its full time of sunshine and rain, and has long patience. A child so often wants to pick the half-ripe fruit; the husbandman knows to wait till the proper time.

Man in his spiritual nature too, is under the law of gradual growth that reigns in all created life. It is only in the path of development that he can reach his divine destiny. And it is the Father, in whose hands are the times and seasons, who alone knows the moment when the soul or the church is ripened to that fullness of faith in which it can really take and keep the blessing.[2]

Prayers Are Never Wasted

Picture an old-fashioned water mill that ground the corn between two huge flat stones. These heavy stones were turned by a water-wheel which moved when there was enough water to fill up the pond and flow over the dam onto the buckets of the wheel. Our praying is like the drops of water that fill the pond so the wheel may turn. The persistent prayer, the shameless prayer, the crying out before God are all like streams of water flowing in. Hence these prayers are not being wasted.

We all know friends who have prayed for years for a wayward child. Maybe you have prayed for months for someone who hates you or for a situation which seems impossible. But we can be assured that no prayers are being wasted. They are filling up the pond and putting more and more pressure against the dam. They are slowly getting ready to slosh over onto that wheel!

Activity behind the Scenes

Murray says God will not delay one moment longer than is absolutely necessary. He will do all in His power to hasten and speed the answer. He is like the farmer who does not harvest the crop too soon because He knows it is far better to wait until it is ripe. He is patient with that crop until just the right time and then, and only then, He brings it in speedily.

> There may be in those around us, there may be in that great system of being of which we are part, there may be in God's government things that have to be put right through our prayer, ere the answer can fully come: the faith that has, according to the command, believed that it has received, can allow God to take His time; it knows it has prevailed and must prevail. In quiet, persistent, and determined perseverance it continues in prayer and thanksgiving until the blessing comes.
>
> Let no delay shake our faith. Of faith it holds good: first the blade, then the ear, then the full corn in the ear. Each believing prayer brings a step nearer the final victory. Each believing prayer helps to ripen the fruit and bring us nearer to it; it fills up the measure of prayer and faith known to God alone; it conquers the hindrances in the unseen world; it hastens the end.

Child of God! Give the Father time. He is long-suffering over you. He wants the blessing to be rich, and full, and sure; give Him time, while you cry day and night. Only remember the word: 'I say unto you, He will avenge them speedily.'[3]

Because of persevering prayers things are happening in the unseen world, in people's personalities, and in the institutional church. Prayer is rearranging some factors.

And yet we still may not have seen those changes take place in our church for which we have been burdened to pray. But take heart and remember that God may not yet be ready to bring about those particular changes until we have prayed long enough for all the component parts to be in place.

An experienced farmer will wait until every part of the growth process is complete and the crop is ripe. In the same way, our continued praying will help get both seen and unseen factors into line so that God's blessing will speedily come in that church. God "bears long" with His people precisely so He can "avenge them speedily."

Time + Prayer = Victory!

Do you remember the elderly Scottish lady? In her case, it took *fifty-three years* before a myriad of factors were brought into the right combination. Fifty-three years passed by as drop by drop, prayer by prayer, the pond filled up, spilled over, and the mighty wheel turned. She prayed on through fifty-three years of God's longsuffering, and yet in the annals of eternity, it will surely be stated that God did, in fact, avenge His elect speedily.

And what we must keep in mind if we are to become "world-changers" is that the prayers of the humble saint who prayed were a potent force in getting everything ready for the great change to happen. The years went on. She and her friend both grew older, but she never lost faith in the promises of God that He will hear and answer prayer.

This faithful Christian would be amazed to find that her persistence is being commended to others! She had simply learned over the years that there is nothing that cannot be effected by prayer, and was an encouragement and example to many who knew her.

We must remember both the human illustrations as well as the words of the Scripture whenever we are tempted to give up praying for something after a few weeks or months! Together they offer the strongest encouragement to believe that God will indeed answer our prayers. It may simply be a question of time.

Your name
shall no longer be called Jacob,
but Israel;
for you have struggled with
God and with men,
and have prevailed.
(Genesis 32:28)

7

WRESTLING IN PRAYER

A nother problem that is closely connected with this matter of perseverance is "wrestling in prayer." There are times when asking and receiving come automatically and easily, but we have all experienced occasions when that does not happen. It takes effort and determination, even "blood, sweat, and tears," for things to change.

Think of John Knox on his deathbed. He literally spent the last two days of his life in this kind of hard battling. He told those anxiously watching over him that in fact he had been fighting against Satan on behalf of the church. Even then, worn out and desperately ill, he did not think that it was time to retire and look forward to rest in heaven!

Or think of how tirelessly some parents will pray and pray for a wayward child until he or she finally gives in to the call of the covenant God to the obedience of faith. That is not the kind of prayer hastily uttered last thing at night, but an example of what the Bible encourages us to emulate if we wish to see answers.

This way of describing persevering prayer comes from the life of the Old Testament patriarch, Jacob, who spent a long night wrestling with an unknown man who turned out to be none other than the Lord Himself! We have already looked briefly at that night of prayer, in the context of discovering that it is legitimate to argue with God on the basis of His own character and glory.

Blessing Ahead

Basic to the theological understanding of prayer is the awareness that God is doing something *in* us (see chapter 3). He is working to get us into a place where we will have power with Him. Could it not be that one of the major reasons that God lets us wrestle in our prayers is that He wants to turn us, in our own particular way and in our own particular circumstances, from a "Jacob" into an "Israel"?

There is no way we can get to that place except by being constrained to spend much time and energy wrestling with Him in prayer. There is a parallel in the time and effort spent in bodybuilding: strength in prayer is truly developed through exertion. God has some tremendous blessings in store for His people in the church as well as for the needy multitudes now in the world. But He cannot, and will not, part with those blessings until we are prepared to wrestle in prayer with Him, long and hard. There is a reason for this.

In a wrestling match, the two sides engage at close quarters. They literally "come to grips with one another." There is no way out of the ring, until one has forced the other to submit. With God, of course, it is a foregone conclusion who is superior! However, it is almost as though He beckons us to "take Him on," challenging us to become closely involved with His purposes on earth, for in wrestling with Him we get close to Him.

Throughout the process, He begins to break us and make changes deep inside us that are necessary before He can turn us into an "Israel." Then He will grant us the kind of power in prayer to say, "Lord, I want that," and hear God reply, "You shall have it."

A Struggle Which Left Jacob Permanently Changed

Genesis 32 and 33 describe the events which made Jacob the *spiritual father* of all who wrestle in prayer until they prevail. His life and experience can offer much insight.

The name Jacob, prophetically given at birth, means *the Supplanter,* and refers to the fact that he would cheat his older brother out of his birthright. But this same man won the name Israel, *Prince with God,* after wrestling successfully with the Lord. He was a completely changed man after that night.

Jacob was returning to his home country after many years' absence. He was bringing his large family with him and was terrified at the thought of facing Esau, his brother, whom he had cheated and mortally offended years before. News came that Esau was coming to meet him with a large group of heavily armed men, and Jacob had no army. What could he do?

Fearing the arrival of the hostile troops next morning, he encamped by the ford of the brook Jabbok. There he spent the whole night alone, wrestling in prayer with God until he got the blessing of divine protection the next day. In fact the text indicates that what happened was that God came to him and physically wrestled with him. That was God's way of drawing him out in prayer. He had to literally fight to win blessing, and relief from the enemy.

Now Jacob was making the best possible preparation for the confrontation he dreaded the next day, because Proverbs 21:1 says, "The King's heart is in the hand of the Lord, like the rivers of water; he turns it wherever he wishes." He was looking to God to act on his behalf. But God called on him to wrestle that night for Esau's heart to be turned. This battle was won in advance in the place of prayer.

But it was still a battle and it cost him something. It took him the whole night — he lost a night's sleep. But more than that, in the struggle, the stranger touched his thigh (which was the way of making a personal binding covenant in the ancient world) — so that Jacob was partially lame for the rest of his life.

Worth the Cost

It was indeed costly for Jacob, but he won the eternal gain. His name was changed that night from Jacob, a constant reminder of his somewhat dishonest character, to Israel, *Prince with God.* And it was not in name only. The story shows that the struggle permanently transformed not only his whole personality, but his authority in prayer.

That is the real reason many of us have to wrestle so hard over so many things and be so deeply grieved and hurt. God takes the initiative with us. He takes us on, as He did Jacob. Though we experience real pain, we can take courage as we become aware that it is in His love and mercy that He is determined to turn us from a Jacob into an Israel. Then we will have our ultimate desire, which is to prevail with Him for the needs of His kingdom and win through bringing glory to His name.

Like Jacob, the change we win through the struggle can be permanent. We will not have to travel exactly the same way twice. Each time will leave us a little more like Jesus, and leave us with a little more power in prayer.

Over the years, every experience of answered prayer will increase our confidence in God's willingness to answer and His power to change things. Remember that God plans to release His blessings eventually, and let nothing deter you until He does. There may well be a cost, but it will ultimately be worth it all.

Setting Our Priorities

Not only in Jacob's experience, but also in ours, it takes hard wrestling with ourselves and with the Lord to be turned from self-centered manipulators into princes with God. Even to begin this kind of wrestling for princely authority in prayer will mean rethinking personal priorities in order to put time with God at the top of the list. We often have to struggle hard with ourselves and many conflicting demands on our time and energy just to get ourselves to the place of beginning to pray. It will not just happen.

For churches to have Israel-like powers of intercession, they must be filled with people whose self-importance has been so broken down that they genuinely realize that everything hinges on God. This God-centered awareness will be daily reflected in the amount of time they now spend before God on their knees in intercession for the world.

Thus the first stage in learning to wrestle through to victory in prayer is to win the battle over ourselves, to shake off our lethargy, so that we set prayer as a number one priority. That will mean constantly reminding ourselves why intercession is so important and then systematically arranging our day in order to give ourselves to this important task.

A Daily Plan

John Calvin in *Institutes of the Christian Religion*, Book III Chapter 20:50, suggested systematic prayer five times a day. He said that we should always pray without ceasing, and since we are so weak that we have to have many helps to strengthen us and are so lazy that we need to be goaded into action, it is fitting that each one of us should set apart certain times for this exercise. Calvin taught that those hours should not pass without prayer, and during them all the devotion of the heart should be completely occupied with it. The five specific hours he had in mind were:

- when we first get up in the morning,
- before we begin our daily work,
- when we sit down to a meal,
- when by God's blessing we have eaten,
- and when we are getting ready to retire.[1]

Feelings!

Another stage in wrestling is the struggle to overcome feelings of uselessness and deadness in prayer. Once we have won the primary battle of making prayer a major priority on our time schedule, then the devil will certainly attack us in the area of feelings about the activity to which we are now giving so much time. "Is it worth it?" he will ask. Indeed, he may go on, "Are *you* worth it? Will a holy God hear an unworthy person like you?"

While feelings do of course have a legitimate place, we cannot afford to depend on them alone when we decide what is right for us to do. It is simply a matter of priority and of duty. A war is not won on whether the army *feels* like fighting! So it is with prayer. Jesus says that those who persevere in prayer do get through to the blessing, regardless of how they feel.

We may well feel extremely unclean and unworthy, but the fact is that we are not coming to God in our own name at all. It does not matter if we are all too aware of sin in our lives that very day, because we come in the name of Jesus whose blood can cleanse us from all sin. Remember, every time we pray we are simply doing what He said to do.

B. M. Palmer, in his *Theology Of Prayer*, has a beautiful passage in which he encourages us not to worry too much about how we feel when we are praying. He looks at the influence of emotions from a different perspective. We may have learned to resist the devil when he reminds us of our sinfulness, but our feelings may trip us up in another way.

We may remember times when the Lord seemed especially real to us, and it was easy to pray. From time to time in our lives there do come special periods when prayer is a deep joy and is blessed with unusual power. But Palmer warns us that Christians are not to expect always to be on a spiritual and emotional "mountaintop." In fact, they could not stand it if they were! With profound psychological insight, he says:

> The wear and tear of strong excitement, if continuous, would destroy life. The sword will cut through the scabbard if too frequently drawn. God has constituted the

emotions like the tides of the sea — now rising to their flood, then ebbing back to the bosom of the deep; or, to employ another analogy, in the reaction which invariably follows unusual excitement, nature provides a repose to the spirit akin to that which sleep affords to the body.[2]

Consider Fasting

A pastor in South Carolina, who was encountering some opposition to the Word, decided that he would attempt to combat the evident work of the evil one not only by prayer, but also by regular fasting. He and his wife noticed that the very day, or within a few days, of his fast the same thing would always happen. There would be a knock on the door of his office, and someone would come in to tell him how God had either just saved them or worked very significantly in their life. This happened too often to be a coincidence.

So when their six-year-old son was giving them some discipline problems, they fasted and prayed for him, too. That night, for the first time in weeks, they felt that they were able to see a significant change in his attitude toward his parents and the things of the Lord.

This couple had discovered, almost by accident, the fact that closely related to this matter of wrestling in prayer — from a Jacob-like condition with the Lord to an Israel-like condition — is the discipline of fasting. In fact, Jesus gave instruction on fasting at the same time He gave them instruction on prayer (see Matthew 6). Later He encouraged his disciples to practice it when faced with apparent failure in their ministry.

When the Lord Jesus Christ came down from the Mount of Transfiguration, where the glory of God had burst through His very face, He found that His disciples in the valley below had a terrible problem. They had not been able to help a child who was tormented with an evil spirit. They found that they were totally unable to cast it out. But when the transfigured, glorious Christ entered that situation where evil was so powerful, He cast out the evil spirit without a moment's hesitation.

His amazed disciples wondered why they had been so powerless to handle the situation. Later when they asked Him privately why they had failed, the Lord immediately responded, "This kind can come out by nothing but prayer and fasting" (Mark 9:29).[3]

Fasting is a way of bringing the powerful Christ down from the mountain of glory into our valley of helplessness to do the work we cannot accomplish. But we must keep this in mind: in proper fasting, the emphasis is never on our merits or on our personal feelings as we fast. Rather we should be solely concerned with bringing down the presence of the risen Christ. The stress should be on God's presence and glory and not at all on ourselves.

Andrew Murray says that prayer and fasting are like two hands. Whenever we pray, it is as though we are reaching out and putting one hand on the mercy seat, the place that symbolized God's forgiving presence on the Ark of the covenant. But when we fast, we take our other hand off the legitimate things of this world (such as the comforts of food) and cast all earthly supports aside in order to put both hands on that mercy seat.[4]

You will understand, of course, that fasting means abstaining from food for a period of time, usually for twenty-four hours in which you spend special time in prayer. Perhaps during the time usually set aside for the three meals, instead of eating you meditate, read the Word, and pray.

Fasting is like a silent prayer: simply turning away from human sustenance, toward the Sustainer of all, is a quiet and real means of beseeching Him to take our need seriously. It signals to God our commitment to Him and our conviction that human means are totally inadequate. We are begging Him to send the presence of Christ.

Extraordinary Power for a Dying World

Although apparently long neglected among evangelical Christians, the crucial discipline of fasting is being taken seriously once again. In the United States, an organization has arisen that calls itself Intercessors for America. Its purpose is to appeal to churches and individuals to fast and pray for repentance and revival the first Friday of every month.

In Great Britain, Intercessors for Britain, a group called the Lydias, and others regularly call for national days of prayer and fasting. Intercessors for Australia do the same thing for Australia on the last Friday of each month. Korean believers have long fasted regularly, and the same is true in many churches of Africa and elsewhere.

The course of future church and world history, in accordance with the unbreakable purposes of God, will be largely determined by how many of God's people join in these and similar calls to fast and pray. We may literally be standing at a crossroads in history.

What will the future hold? There seems to be a choice between a totalitarian, humanist future for the nations and one of developing freedom with increasing influence of Christianity. What ultimately happens may well hang upon the intercession, perseverance, wrestling, and fasting of countless, uncredited, unacknowledged people of God.

Can any compassionate believer possibly justify not joining these multitudes on their knees? The hymn of Charlotte Elliott is straight to the point:

> Watch, as if on that alone
> Hung the issue of the day:
> Pray, that help may be sent down:
> Watch and pray.

Shall not the judge
of all the earth
do right?
(Genesis 18:25)

8

WHEN GOD APPEARS
TO SAY NO

What are we supposed to think about the case of someone who would seem to fulfill every condition of Christlikeness, who for years had learned the disciplines of wrestling and persevering in prayer, but yet who, in their last days, lay powerless and wracked with pain? This is exactly what happened to the remarkable missionary to South India, Amy Carmichael.

She spent her life in the service of orphans, many saved from a life of prostitution in Hindu temples, and built up a marvelous village and training center for them that lasts to this day. Her spiritual wisdom and influence was enormous, and over and over again, God heard and miraculously answered the prayers of the community.

In many respects, one would say that prayer was the hallmark of her life and ministry. The place was literally founded and run on prayer. But these final prayers for her healing, He never answered. Why?

Divine Denial or Something Better

To deal honestly with the theological and practical problems that are raised by the Biblical teaching on prayer, we must consider this one final problem which is not dealt with by the observations already made regarding perseverance and wrestling. What indeed shall we think about divine denials of our petitions?

I do not mean things that we pray about for thirty years and then do receive after hard perseverance. Rather, I have in mind those things to which God clearly says, "No, my beloved child, you shall not have this."

And of course I am not referring to God's denial of openly wicked things, but of things that, from our human point of view, might well accord with His will and glory. Sometimes no doubt we have started to pray for something we were not sure was in God's will. Nevertheless, we continued sincerely and persevered with our request, and yet He said no.

Calvin gives us the proper clue to understanding at least part of the difficulty here. He says in *Institutes* III.20:52

Besides, even if God grants our prayer, he does not always respond to the exact form of our request but rather seems to hold us in suspense. Nevertheless, in a remarkable way, he eventually shows us our prayers have not been in vain. This is what John's words mean: "And if we know that He hears us, whatever we ask, we know that we have the petitions that we have asked of Him" (1 John 5:15).

Now this may seem to be rather a repetitive collection of words! But the assertion in fact is extremely practical, because it tells us that God, even when he does not comply with our wishes, is still attentive and kindly disposed towards our prayers. This means that any hope based upon his word will never disappoint us. So believers need to be patient, sustained by this truth, since they could not stand for very long if they did not rely upon it.

B. M. Palmer says in one of his sermons that those things which we have been pleading for are not ultimately denied by God.[1] Instead, He gives us the true underlying intention of our prayer, which was whatever the Holy Spirit was asking for within us.

Our mistake was that we interpreted the restriction He placed on our wants as being something denied us! Yet the real blessing was conveyed in another form which perhaps prevented danger or trouble that would have occurred if we had received it in the form we first requested.

Temporary Suffering

The great Southern Presbyterian theologian, John L. Girardeau, had to face this problem when he returned from the Confederate army to a defeated and depressed Charleston. Many wondered why God had refused to honor their ceaseless prayers to grant the South its independence. So Girardeau felt led to preach a series on prayer. Introducing the printed edition of these sermons, he wrote:

> Daily prayer was offered by crowds of worshipers for the success of the Confederate struggle. In consequence of its disastrous result, many of God's people were, by Satanic influence, tempted to slack their confidence in prayer. These sermons were an humble attempt to help them under this trial.[2]

Speaking of God's mysterious denial of some of the legitimate supplications (at least from the human viewpoint) of His people, the great preacher states:

> He may suffer them, for wise purposes, to undergo apparent defeat, and to be exposed to a tempest of opprobrium, oppression and scorn. In these cases it is our duty to sustain ourselves by the consideration that God does His will, and that the Judge of all the earth will do right.
>
> And to him who thus in disappointment and suffering, baffled in his hopes, and tempted to skepticism, yet honors God by a meek and uncomplaining submission due from a sinful, short-sighted creature, to infinite wisdom and absolute sovereignty, it will in time be made conspicuously to appear—as clearly as the flash of a sunbeam through the fissures of a dissolving cloud—that benefits were withheld for the bestowal of greater, that temporary suffering is but the prelude to everlasting blessing, short-lived disappointment to the dawn of unfading honor, and that truth and right go down beneath a horizon of darkness and an ocean of storms, only to reappear in the morning glory of an eternal triumph.
>
> Jesus as an infirm, dying human being, staggering under the curse of a world, prayed that He might be delivered from suffering the second death. His prayer was unanswered and He died; but His grave was the scene of death's dethronement and the birth place of unnumbered millions of deathless souls redeemed from Satan, sin and hell.
>
> Hold, Christian brother! Do not despair because your prayers for certain blessings . . . have for a time been unanswered. Where is your faith? Where is your allegiance to your almighty, all-wise, all-merciful Sovereign? Collect yourself. Put on the panoply of God . . . Look up. God, your redeemer and deliverer, reigns.

See, He sits on yonder throne, and suns and systems of light are but the sparkling dust beneath His feet. Thousands of thousands of shining seraphs minister before Him. Infinite empire is in His grasp. . . . His eye is upon His afflicted people.

See, see, He comes, He comes, riding upon the wings of the whirlwind, wielding His glittering sword bathed in the radiance of heaven, driving His foes like chaff before His face, and hastening to the succor of His saints with resources of boundless power and illimitable grace.[3]

Would these words not have brought some encouragement to Girardeau's congregation? His people would surely have wondered why God had brought them revival several years before, in answer to prayer, but had apparently not answered their prayers at all during the war. So we find that in the end it is a question of *perspective*.

The correct perspective helps us to keep praying. Because the desire for God's glory and for the church's welfare, which motivates our specific requests, is a God given desire, it will always be honored. Even when God says no to one of our requests, He still uses our holy desires and our acts of praying to bring in His kingdom, accomplish His will, and to provide for, pardon, and protect His people. Looking at it this way, we understand that when God says no, He is still saying yes but in a higher, more mysterious way than we first thought. Temporary setbacks should not discourage us, because there is every reason to continue in the mighty work of intercession.

In the Gap

And yet this ministry of intercession is extremely demanding, because it demands our whole selves. It takes untold wrestling before we can fully experience the transformation from being a powerless, self-seeking Jacob to experiencing prevailing power in prayer because God has made us a prince with Himself.

He can only grant us such authority when, like Jacob, we have been through the kind of struggle which issues in personal brokenness. If Jacob limped for the rest of his life, we should not be surprised if we permanently bear the marks of God's hand in our lives. But look what it accomplished in him! No one else in Scripture was honored by God with such a title!

How can we, too, move beyond our self-centeredness in prayer? How can we follow the pattern for prayer given by the Son of God? How can we truly put Him first, hallow His name, and bring about His sovereign plan here on earth?

What will it take to develop in us the maturity and conformity to Christ that we need in order to be heard at all? Where will we find the stamina, as individuals or as churches, to persevere on behalf of others with desperate needs?

With Jesus

Power in prayer is found not by looking at ourselves, but by concentrating on the one with whom and through whom and for whom we wrestle. Instead of fainting, we need to keep looking to Jesus, who will enable us to win the battle of intercession.

The devil will do all he can to keep Christians from realizing this crucial principle for spiritual warfare: it is because we look to Jesus that we actually get through to the Father and have our intercession prevail with Him. As long as the evil one can cause us to keep our eyes on ourselves and to be preoccupied with how well or how poorly we are doing, then he keeps our intercessory power as weak as Samson when his hair was cut by Delilah!

But look at what happens when Christians get their eyes off themselves and onto the right person: they begin to intercede with mighty power that changes things, first in heaven and then on earth!

A wonderful illustration of how identification with Christ causes believers to win the battle of intercession is related by Dr. Robert L. Dabney in his biography of the great Confederate general from Virginia, Thomas J. "Stonewall" Jackson.[4]

"Stonewall" Jackson was accidentally shot by his own troops in 1863 during the tragic War Between the States. His body was laid in state in the Capitol in Richmond, Virginia for two days before his funeral at his home Presbyterian Church in Lexington. Tens of thousands of mourning Confederate people crowded into the Capitol building during those short days to look on their beloved slain leader for the last time.

As the sun was setting on the last day of viewing, the marshall gave orders for the great doors of the Senate chamber to be closed. Hundreds of sad people would thus be excluded from paying their last tribute. Just before the gates were finally shut, a rough looking Confederate veteran in tattered gray uniform pushed and shoved his way forward, tears running down his bearded cheeks.

The marshall in charge was about to push this insistent old man down the steps, when suddenly he lifted up the stump of his right arm, and cried out, "By this right arm, which I gave for my country, I demand the right of seeing my general one more time!" The governor of the Commonwealth of Virginia happened to be standing nearby and ordered the marshall to let the old veteran in with these words, "He has won entrance by his wounds."

His Wounds Win Entrance for Us

In a somewhat similar, and yet infinitely more wonderful way, believers in Jesus win entrance to the Father's favorable presence by way of the wounds of the Savior, received in His victorious struggles on Calvary on our behalf. Revelation 5:6 speaks of the reigning Lord in glory as a "Lamb . . . [that] had been slain."

Evidently even in His glorified resurrection body, He still bears the marks of our salvation upon Him. Every time we pray in Jesus name, it is as though the Father looks upon the wounds of the Son and says: His wounds have won you continual entrance into My throne room. Make your request known!

That is how we can continually experience the strength to join Christ "in the gap" as intercessors. We must remember that the Lamb who was slain is also the risen, conquering Lion of Judah. His wounds give us entrance to the Father, and the continuing prayers of His risen life give us protection and make us fruitful in our earthly pilgrimage for Him. This is the one who is interceding for us in all our weakness.

However, He is not only before the throne on our behalf. When we commit ourselves to stand "in the gap," we

find that He is already there in the place of intercession.
We are actually joining Him who is our supernatural life
and strength.

I end with a poem quoted by Palmer in his *Theology
Of Prayer*. The unknown author is imagining what the
Son says to the Father when a humble Christian, someone like you or me, brings a stumbling prayer to the
heavenly throne. Yes, we have sinned. Yes, we do not
know how to pray as we should. But Jesus is standing in
the gap for us and with us. He is the secret source of our
own strength to struggle through to victory in the mighty
battle of intercession.

THE INTERCESSOR

Father, I bring this worthless child to thee,
To claim thy pardon once, yet once again.
Receive him at my hands, for he is mine.
He is a worthless child; he owns his guilt.
Look not on him; he cannot bear thy glance.
Look thou on me; his vileness I will hide.
He pleads not for himself, he dares not plead.
His cause is mine, I am his Intercessor.

By each pure drop of blood I lost for him,
By all the sorrows graven on my soul,
By every wound I bear, I claim it due.
Father divine! I cannot have him lost.
He is a worthless soul, but he is mine.
Sin hath destroyed him; sin hath died in me.
Death hath pursued him; I have conquer'd death.
Satan hath bound him; Satan is my slave.

My Father! hear him now — not him, but me.
I would not have him lost for all the world
Thou for my glory hast ordain'd and made,
Because he is a poor and contrite child,

And all, his every hope, on me reclines.
I know my children, and I know him mine;
By all the tears he weeps upon my bosom,
By his full heart that beateth against mine;

I know him by his sighings and his prayers,
By his deep, trusting love, which clings to me.
I could not bear to see him cast away,
Weak as he is, the weakest of my flock,
The one that grieves me most, that moves me least.

I measure not my love by his returns,
And though the stripes I send to speed him home
Drive him upon the instant from my breast,
Still he is mine; I drew him from the world;
He has no right, no home, but in my love.
Though earth and hell against his soul conspire,
I shield him, keep him, save him; we are one.[5]

A SUGGESTED PLAN FOR BIBLE READING

S ince our prayers are so directly fed by the promises
and patterns of God's written Word, the age-old practice of reading a portion of Scripture each day as a preparation for prayer is surely a wise one. We have seen the
power of prayer; now we will consider the power of the
Word.

Letting Loose a Lion

The great English preacher of last century, Charles Spurgeon, used to speak of preaching the Bible as "letting a
lion loose." While the preached Word is indeed special
(particularly, as we have said, when it is backed up by the
congregational prayer meeting), our own reading can have
a profound effect on us as individuals. To understand the
message of the Word of God is indeed to let loose forces
in our lives as powerful as a lion. Look at what it has done
in history.

When the Scottish Parliament passed a law in 1543 making it legal for the people to read the Word of God in English, a "lion was let loose" that would never be shut up. In his *History of the Reformation,* John Knox comments that publishing the Bible in English made the religious revival, which we call the Reformation, possible and inevitable. He speaks about the year 1543:

> Then might have been seen the Bible lying almost upon every gentleman's table. The New Testament was borne about in many men's hands. . . . thereby did the knowledge of God wondrously increase, and God give His Holy Spirit to simple men in great abundance. (vol. I, p. 45)

The Bible—with the blessing of the Holy Spirit—brought revival and reformation to sixteenth-century Scotland and to all Northern Europe, and since that time has continued to bring salvation and new life to individuals and nations. Imagine what a thorough knowledge of it could do in your life and your church! And think how it could be used to fuel a prayer life shaped by an informed grasp of the revealed will of God.

Here is another, more recent example of the power of the Word. After the Marxists took over Russia in the 1917 revolution, they began printing anti-Christian tracts by the millions. These tracts quoted portions of Scripture in order to ridicule it and point out mistakes in it.

However, the printing presses were soon brought to a screeching halt when the government realized that thousands of people were being converted to Christ just by reading these little "chopped up" portions of God's Word in tracts that were intended to destroy religion! Unwittingly, the communist authorities had let a lion loose!

But what shall we read and in what order? The most basic answer is this: we need to read the whole Bible on a regular and systematic basis. We need to become familiar with the whole Word in order to get the whole message that God has for His people.

Since God, in His wise providence, inspired in an infallible and inerrant manner all sixty-six books of Scripture, He must have something very important to tell us in every part of the book which He so carefully superintended. If we do not read all parts of Scripture on a regular basis, then we will miss out on some things we need to know.

Or to put it another way, Christ speaks to us in all parts of His Word. To have the wholeness and fullness of Christ in us, we need the entirety of the Word. What the Rev. William Still of Aberdeen, Scotland, says about preaching, we could say about Bible reading: "If you do not teach the whole Word to your people, both you and they will go astray commensurately to the extent and importance of your omissions: e.g. a Christian needs the book of Proverbs and the epistle of Philemon as well as Genesis, the Psalms, and Isaiah, the Gospels . . ."[1]

There is no reason why most Christians cannot read through the Bible once every year, if they take it in manageable portions day by day. But how can we get through the whole Bible once a year without becoming bogged down in genealogies, battles, or tabernacle instructions?

A Daily Portion

The following simple plan was passed on to me by an outstanding and consecrated Lumbee Indian preacher, Venus Brooks, of Pembroke, North Carolina. It has been helpful to many since Puritan times and was designed to cover the Scriptures in exactly 365 days.

Its special value is that it gives you a varied diet by exposing you to different parts of Scripture each day while providing continuity by causing you to return to the same section on the same day of the week all through the year. There is a further advantage in that it also helps you see the wonderful unity and remarkable interconnections of various sections of Scripture. For instance, a quotation that you read on Sunday in Psalms, may be picked up on Saturday in Hebrews.

- *Sunday*: read 5 chapters in Psalms (and then go on to the following books: Proverbs, Ecclesiastes, The Song of Solomon).

- *Monday*: read 3 chapters in Genesis (and the following books: Exodus, Leviticus, Numbers, Deuteronomy).

- *Tuesday*: read 3 chapters in Joshua (and the following books: Judges, Ruth, 1 Samuel, 2 Samuel, 1 Kings, 2 Kings).

- *Wednesday*: read 3 chapters in Job (after finishing Job, then go to the following books: 1 Chronicles, 2 Chronicles, Ezra, Nehemiah, Esther).

- *Thursday*: read 3 chapters in Isaiah (and the following books: Jeremiah, Lamentations, Ezekiel, Daniel, Hosea, Joel, Amos, Obadiah, Jonah, Micah, Nahum, Habakkuk, Zephaniah, Haggai, Zechariah, Malachi).

- *Friday*: read 3 chapters in Matthew (and the following books: Mark, Luke, John, Acts).

- *Saturday*: read 3 chapters in Romans (and the following books: 1 Corinthians, 2 Corinthians, Galatians, Ephesians, Philippians, Colossians, 1 Thessalonians,

2 Thessalonians, 1 Timothy, 2 Timothy, Titus, Philemon, Hebrews, James, 1 Peter, 2 Peter, 1 John, 2 John, 3 John, Jude, Revelation).

In order to keep up with where you are from week to week, you will need to have a marker for each section. Keep your place with these in each of the seven sections. Then each day when you come to the end of the section that you read, make some kind of mark in your Bible, so that you will know exactly where to begin when you come back to it on the same day the following week.

Toward the end of the year, you will find that you complete some of the sections before others, because they are not all exactly the same length. Then just transfer your marker to one of the longer sections, and read from that section on two or more days a week until you are through.

Water of Life

So how can the *lion-like* power of God's Word be let loose in my own daily life? As with prayer, for devotions to become a regular part of our daily lives, we need to keep in the front of our minds a vision of who God is.

The last chapter of the Bible speaks of "a pure river of water of life, clear as crystal, proceeding from the throne of God and of the Lamb" (Revelation 22:1). We saw at the beginning of our study of prayer that the books of Revelation and of John speak often of God in terms of life and light and love. Thus Revelation 22 paints us a picture of the life and light and love of God flowing down to us like a river of water.

How can these streams of living water reach us? The answer is that they break forth through the Scriptures and flood the place of prayer for those who make daily devotions a number one priority. If you are not convinced that this is true, at least try it and you will find a supernatural atmosphere coming into your life and things happening which you would never have anticipated

For example, you will find that your mind is filled more and more with thoughts of God, and that your perspective on life begins to change. Days no longer slip by without a thought of Jesus. You begin to pray when matters get hard to handle, instead of complaining, and you begin to recognize the hand of God at work when things do change. Praise wells up in your heart as you become increasingly alert to His blessings.

The Right Attitude

One of the finest guides to life-transforming Bible reading is found in Question 90 of the *Westminster Shorter Catechism:*

> Q: How is the Word to be read and heard, that it may become effectual to salvation?
> A: That the Word may become effectual to salvation, we must attend thereunto with diligence, preparation, and prayer; receive it with faith and love, lay it up in our hearts, and practice it in our lives.

To have the blessings of the Word of God loose in our lives, the first thing we must do is to "attend it with diligence." To attend to the Word is very much like a waitress in a restaurant waiting on people at a table. She pays very close attention to them so she can get their exact order and

convey it to the kitchen. If we are going to get our orders
from Scripture, we have to study it closely and open wide
the ears of our understanding so we can take down its specific directions.

Dr. Alexander Whyte of Edinburgh, graphically illustrated what it means to pay diligent attention. He used to
tell his congregation to imagine someone craning their
neck far over to one side in order to get their ear as close
as possible to the speaker, because they could not bear to
lose a single word he said! If we come to the Scriptures
with the attitude that something very important is going to
be said to us that we do not want to miss, then an atmosphere of reverence and expectation is created, that clears
the air for rich messages from the throne of God.

How different from a perfunctory reading of Scripture
while the television is blaring, two children are talking to
me at the same time, and my mind is a hundred miles
away making plans for next week's trip! When we read
the Word of God, we are to come in a quiet, reverent, and
expectant attitude which will honor the Holy Spirit's presence rather than grieve Him and drive Him away. Ultimately, He is the one who must convey the message, and
so to pay close attention to the Word is a way of honoring
and loving Him, the one who originally inspired the text.

Proper Preparation

"To attend it with preparation" simply means that we are
to prepare ourselves to study the Word of God. Obviously,
the new birth is an essential preparation for understanding
the Scriptures, for "the natural man does not receive the
things of the Spirit of God, for they are foolishness to him;

nor can he know them, because they are spiritually discerned" (1 Corinthians 2:14).

When the Holy Spirit brings us to the birth in Christ, He pours light into our minds so that we can see and understand the truths of the Word; He unstops our ears so that we can hear the voice of the Good Shepherd speaking in the Scriptures. Yet wonderful and essential as it is, the new birth does not guarantee that each time we open the Bible we are prepared sufficiently to study the Scriptures.

Since the Scriptures were written in another age and culture, and since the different parts of Scripture refer to and depend upon one another, it takes continual study on our part to be better and better prepared to understand exactly what (in the words of the Larger Catechism, Question 157) "the matter and scope" of the text means. Bible handbooks, good commentaries, the Westminster Confession of Faith, and perhaps most of all, the preaching of faithful pastors, can help us be prepared to interpret rightly the Word of God.

Approach God's Word with Prayer

But there is something even more essential than study to open our lives to take in the Word of God: all of our Bible reading must be bathed in prayer. John Calvin regularly prayed the following prayer before giving his Bible lectures:

> May the Lord grant that we may contemplate the mysteries of His heavenly wisdom with truly increasing devotion, to His glory and to our edification. Amen.

We would do well to pray such a prayer before our private Bible reading. And yet for Bible reading to teem with life, we must do far more than pray an opening prayer.

We must pray all through the reading: we must turn appropriate parts of the reading into prayer. If you want to know more about how to turn the promises of God into prayer, then read *The Life of Elijah* by A. W. Pink. In a practical and inspiring way, Pink shows us through the experiences of Elijah how to pray according to the promises.

Eager Anticipation

After Adam and Eve had sinned in the Garden of Eden, they hid from God and heard His voice with terror. But because of the death of Jesus in our place, and because we have been brought into His resurrection life "we also rejoice in God through our Lord Jesus Christ, through whom we have now received the reconciliation" (Romans 5:11). Instead of fleeing an angry God, we eagerly look forward to meeting a loving, reconciled Father with messages of personal kindness and grace in the pages of His holy Word.

I often think of this matter of anticipation in this way. After we were engaged, my fiancee and I were separated by the Atlantic Ocean for several months while she finished her studies in Britain. How eagerly I looked forward to her letters! I received them with love. If we receive the Word of God with this attitude, what blessings will be in store for us and for those around us!

The Value of Memorization

It is no surprise that the Catechism teaches the value of memorizing the Scriptures. This is not just for children: we should continue memorizing portions of Scripture all of our adult lives. We can select verses from our daily reading that have really spoken to us. Alternatively there are many plans that can be followed, such as those laid out by the Navigators or the Bible Memory Association.

The pastor of our own church recently preached through 1 Corinthians 13. He advised the congregation to memorize this great love chapter. Our family did so each night before supper. One day I was tempted more than once to act in an unloving way. Suddenly these words jumped to the front of my mind: "Love suffers long . . . is not provoked." How I blessed God for encouraging me to take the high road through His Word which had been laid up in my heart!

Ultimately, we memorize Scripture because it can then become a deep part of our thinking, and "As [a man] thinks in his heart, so is he" (Proverbs 23:7). What better way for our prayers to be conformed to the will of God! And what a rich store of promises we could lay up to plead with their Giver as a foundation for prayer!

Worth the Effort

Bible reading is not always straightforward. Like prayer, it may sometimes take a struggle to get to grips with all that God has placed there for us. But remember this: God has predestinated us and called us to Christ so that our lives will bear fruit (see John 15:16). The Holy Spirit empowers believers not only to hear the Word, but to be doers of it (see James 1:22).

One of the basic laws of the kingdom is that he who is "faithful over a few things [will be made] ruler over many things" (Matthew 25:23). After we have faithfully carried out the simple things God tells us to do in His Word, He will, in His own good time, show us deeper things. It is the same principle of maturity which we have already studied: we must be faithful in the kindergarten before God can put us into the university! May God grant us faithfulness in Bible reading as well as prayer.

A SUGGESTED PLAN
FOR PRAYER

After having read a daily portion of Scripture (as suggested in Appendix A, or in some other appropriate manner), it is time to turn the promises into prayer. This takes time, planning, and effort.

Be Systematic

Some believers will be able to spend an hour each day in specific prayer. For those of you that wish to try this, Dick Eastman suggests a plan to divide an hour into twelve portions of five minutes each.[1] During each one you cover a different aspect of prayer, thus making an hour much easier to get through.

For my own part, I have made an adaptation of Eastman's method into seven segments: praise, waiting, confession, scripture praying, watching, intercession, and thanksgiving. Each one is perhaps five minutes each, except for intercession, which lasts for perhaps ten to fifteen minutes.

At the end of this appendix you will find several pages to assist you in organizing your time in this way, if you wish. At the top of each page there are suggestions, based largely on Eastman's work, as to how to spend your time. The rest of the space is blank, for your own notes, such as relevant Bible verses, specific items for prayer, encouraging thoughts, or matters and names for intercession.

Long-Term Value

If we are too busy to consider giving this forty to sixty minutes (or some portion of it) to God, let us say four or five times a week, then we may possibly be busier than He wants us to be, and our busyness could ultimately become counterproductive.

There will be many days when you cannot spend as much time as you would like, so that variations in time and approach are fully legitimate. But if you do have something like this as a basic goal, you may be pleasantly surprised at the order and blessing it brings into your life and into the lives of others far and near.

Over the years, you will find that these ten or fifteen minutes of systematically reading the Word, followed by thirty-five or forty minutes of planned prayer, are the best, most powerful, and fruitful hours of this short pilgrim life that you spend on earth. They chart your course and set your compass. They make the efforts of your working hours lastingly effective.

In addition, they release the graces and gifts of the Holy Spirit within you and bring down the blessings of God upon those around you. Most of all, they keep you in tune with and bring joy to the heart of Him who loved you and gave Himself for you.

A Forty-Five Minute Outline for Prayer

Praise (five minutes)

Mentally and verbally honor God for who He is and for what He has done. This is where the Lord's Prayer starts: "Hallowed be Your name." (See Chapter 2 for more details on the praise of God). The Psalms are a great repository of praise. At times it may be appropriate to start off by singing: you could use some hymn of praise that you know, or even better, find an actual psalm — praise inspired by God Himself — in your hymnbook that has been made into verse and set to music.

_____

_____

_____

_____

_____

_____

_____

_____

_____

_____

_____

_____

_____

_____

_____

_____

_____

_____

Waiting (five minutes)

Be still before the Lord (see Psalm 62) and seek to appropriate His presence. Like Brother Lawrence (see Chapter
2), lift your eyes up to the Lord and speak of your love for
Him. Above all, ask the Holy Spirit to help you to concentrate your attention upon the Lord. From time to time it
might be well to read a brief devotional chapter during this
segment of waiting (such as one of the thirty-one chapters
of Andrew Murray's *Waiting On God*).[2]

_____

_____

_____

_____

_____

_____

_____

_____

_____

_____

_____

_____

_____

_____

_____

_____

_____

_____

_____

Confession (five minutes)

Remember that you are in the holy presence of the God who "desire[s] truth in the inward parts" (Psalm 51:6). From time to time pray through Psalm 51 or Psalm 32 or Psalm 139. Be very honest and specific about your sins. Confess them, name them specifically in order humbly but gladly to claim such promises as 1 John 1:9. Pray the simple prayer that John Calvin often prayed at the end of his sermons: "Lord, help us to hate our sins enough to turn from them." Seek a fresh communication of His Spirit to give you power to overcome temptation (1 Corinthians 10:13).

_____

_____

_____

_____

_____

_____

_____

_____

_____

_____

_____

_____

_____

_____

_____

_____

_____

_____

Scripture Praying (five minutes)

Take portions of Scripture (or patterns of God's dealings revealed in the Word) and ask God to apply them in your life and in the situations for which you are concerned. In the words we quoted earlier from C. H. Spurgeon, say to the Lord, "Do as thou hast said!"

What you read before you turned to prayer will often be of some assistance in this process. Just remember, God loves His Word, and when you turn His Word into prayer, He is hearing His own voice, and that voice will have a good reception in heaven above!

_____

_____

_____

_____

_____

_____

_____

_____

_____

_____

_____

_____

_____

_____

_____

_____

_____

_____

Watching (five minutes)

Seek to be alert to what is going on around you in the spiritual and material world. Try to understand reality in terms such as those of Ephesians 6, which describes Christian warfare and armor. Enter into the battle and pray for the defeat of Satan and his evil influences both in your own life and in that of the church. Pray for a fresh "binding of the strong man" that his goods may be spoiled, that precious souls may be brought out from under his sway into the glorious liberty of the children of God (see Matthew 12:29).

Think of the current local, national, and international news events from this perspective. Remember how Daniel's prayers caused a battle to be won in heaven. This is a good example of what *watching* means.

_____

_____

_____

_____

_____

_____

_____

_____

_____

_____

_____

_____

_____

Intercession (fifteen minutes)

Here it is very important to be specific. If people ask you to pray for them, then by all means keep some kind of written prayer list. Write down their name, their specific need, and the date. If and when you find out that the request has been answered, then thank the Lord for a few days and scratch it off your list to make room for others.

Keep missionary letters in order to turn them into prayer. Have access to some kind of world map, so that you may pray systematically for the various countries of the world over the weeks. Keep a definite list of your own needs and those of your various family members. Pray specifically for church, school, business, and state. Pray for revival. And never forget to pray for your enemies. Enough prayer for them in some cases may well turn them into friends!

_____

_____

_____

_____

_____

_____

_____

_____

_____

_____

_____

_____

_____

_____

Thanksgiving (five minutes)

Thank God for His wonderful triune existence and for His infinite goodness to His church in general, as well as you in particular. Thank Him for something He has done in the last day or two. Thank Him for what His Word says He is going to do. Again, be specific and particular. As the old gospel hymn says:

> Count your many blessings;
> Name them one by one,
> Count your many blessings,
> See what God has done.

_____

_____

_____

_____

_____

_____

_____

_____

_____

_____

_____

_____

_____

_____

_____

_____

_____

_____

_____

END NOTES

INTRODUCTION

1. O. Hallesby, *Prayer* (London: Inter-Varsity Fellowship, 1963).

2. Excerpts from a speech given in a Christian Theological Training Center in Tokyo, Japan in 1987.

CHAPTER 1: PRAYER DEPENDS ON WHO GOD IS

1. Richard de St. Victor, *De Trinitate: texte critique avec introduction, notes et tables*. Edited by Jean Ribaillier (Paris: 1958). For an English translation of Book 3 of *The Trinity* see *The Classics of Western Spirituality*, "Richard of St. Victor." Translation and introduction by Grover A. Zinn (New York: Paulist Press, 1979).

2. "The Shepherd of Hermas," in *The Ante-Nicene Fathers*, Vol 2 (Grand Rapids: Eerdmans, 1975).

3. Hallesby, *Prayer*.

CHAPTER 2: PRAYER AND THE PRAISE OF GOD

1. John Calvin, *Commentaries on the Epistle of Paul the Apostle to the Hebrews*. Translated by John Owen (Grand Rapids: Baker Book House, 1979 reprint).

2. Hallesby, *Prayer*.

3. John Calvin, *Institutes of the Christian Religion*, ed. John McNeill, (Philadelphia: Westminster Press, 1960). This quotation has been retranslated for clarity.

4. Brother Lawrence, *The Practice of the Presence of God*. Translation and introduction by E. M. Blaiklock (London: Hodder & Stoughton, 1986).

5. B.M. Palmer, *The Theology of Prayer* (Harrisonburg, VA: Sprinkle Publications, 1980 reprint), 133, 134.

6. Quoted by Dick Eastman, *The Hour That Changes the World*: Baker Book House, p.23.

7. Jonathan Edwards, *Charity and Its Fruits* (London: Banner of Truth Trust, 1969 reprint).

CHAPTER 3: PRAYER AND THE PURPOSES OF GOD

1. See B.B. Warfield, *The Plan of Salvation* (Philadelphia: Presbyterian Board of Publication, 1918).

2. Jacob Burckhardt, *Civilization of the Renaissance in Italy*, Vol. II, chapter IV (New York: Harper & Row Publishers, 1958).

3. Thomas Carlyle, *On Heroes, Hero-Worship* (London: Chapman and Hall, Ltd. 1872, 1897), 134, 135.

4. C. S. Lewis, *The Horse and His Boy* (New York: Macmillan, 1988).

5. Hallesby, *Prayer.*

6. A. W. Pink, *The Beatitudes and the Lord's Prayer* (Grand Rapids: Baker Book House, 1979, 1982), 100, 101.

7. Palmer, *The Theology of Prayer*, 140, 141.

8. Ibid., 141.

9. Ibid., 318-20.

10 Quoted in Eastman, *The Hour That Changes the World*, 88.

CHAPTER 4: PRAYER CHANGES US

1. A. N. Renwick, *Story of the Scottish Reformation* (Grand Rapids: Wm. B. Eerdmans Publishing Co., 1960), 169.

2. Thomas M'Crie, *Life of John Knox* (Edinburgh and London: William Blackwood and Sons, 1880), 35.

3. Sermon on Ephesians 5:32, CO 51: 768, 769.

4. Commentary on 1 John 4.14.

5. John Calvin, *Institutes*, 851. This quotation has been retranslated for clarity.

6. Quoted in Eastman, *The Hour That Changes the World*, 56, 57. Also note that one of the finest books on praying according to the promises, is A. W. Pink's *Life of Elijah* (London: The Banner of Truth Trust, 1968).

7. Edith Schaeffer, *The Tapestry* (Waco, TX: Word Books, 1981).

8. see George Mueller, *Answers to Prayer*. Compiled by A. E. C. Brooks (Chicago: Moody Press, n.d.).

9. Mueller, *Answers to Prayer*.

10. A. T. Robertson, *Word Pictures in the New Testament*, Vol. 1 (Nashville: Sunday School Board of the Southern Baptist Convention, 1930).

CHAPTER 5: PRAYER CHANGES OTHERS

1. George A. Blackburn, ed., *The Life Work of John L. Girardeau* (Columbia, South Carolina: The State Company, 1916), 99, 100.

2. S. D. Gordon, *Quiet Talks on Prayer* (New York: Fleming H. Revell Co., 1904).

3. Blackburn, *The Life Work of John L. Girardeau,* 66, 67.

4. See William Still, *The Work of the Pastor*, 3rd ed. (Aberdeen, Scotland: Gilcomston Church South, 1984). Also the introduction to *The Letters of William Still*, (Edinburgh: Banner of Truth Trust, 1984), 28–30.

5. Since 1945 there has been a growing movement among many congregations of the Church of Scotland, largely under the inspiration of the Rev. William Still of Gilcomston South Parish Church, Aberdeen, to concentrate the ministry and outreach of the church on expository preaching three times a week (Sunday morning, Sunday evening, and Wednesday evening). All of this is specifically backed up and impelled out by a prayer meeting that lasts for between one and two hours every Saturday night! They pray systematically and fervently for the needs of the congregation, wider church connection, nation, mission field, and world.

6. As quoted by Dick Eastman, *No Easy Road* (Grand Rapids: Baker Book House, 1978), 123.

CHAPTER 6: THE CHALLENGE TO PERSEVERE

1. Andrew Murray, *With Christ in the School of Prayer* (Old Tappan, NJ: Fleming H. Revell Company, 1972).

2. Ibid., 87, 88, 89.

3. Ibid., 88.

CHAPTER 7: WRESTLING IN PRAYER

1. At the end of the book, we suggest some simple and systematic ways to approach daily intercessory prayer and Bible reading.

2. B. M. Palmer, *Theology of Prayer*, 164, 165.

3. Some ancient manuscripts of the New Testament are lacking this text, but it is included in the majority of textual witnesses. At any rate, fasting is integral to both Old and New Testaments.

4. Andrew Murray, *With Christ in the School of Prayer*.

CHAPTER 8: WHEN GOD APPEARS TO SAY NO

1. B.M. Palmer, *Sermons*, Vol. II (New Orleans: Clark and Hofeline, 1876), 293. See also 211.

2. George A. Blackburn, ed., *Sermons by John L. Girardeau* (Columbia, South Carolina: The State Company, 1907), 254.

3. Ibid., 264, 265.

4. Robert L. Dabney, *Life and Campaigns of Lt. General Thomas J. Jackson (Stonewall Jackson)* (Harrisonburg, VA: Sprinkle Publications, 1976 reprint).

5. Palmer, *Sermons*, Vol. II, 266.

APPENDIX A

1. Still, *The Work of the Pastor*. Also see "A Charge to Students" in *A Symposium from Past Issues of the TSF Bulletin* (London: The Theological Students' Fellowship, 1964).

APPENDIX B

1. Eastman, *The Hour that Changes the World*.

2. Andrew Murray, *Waiting On God* (London: James Nisbet & Co. Limited, 1901).

ABOUT THE AUTHOR

Douglas Kelly was born in Lumberton, North Carolina. He earned a Bachelor of Arts in Modern Languages from the University of North Carolina at Chapel Hill, a *Diplome de langue et civilisation francaises* from the University of Lyon, France, a Master of Divinity from Union Theological Seminary, Richmond, Virginia, and a Doctor of Philosophy in Systematic Theology from Edinburgh University, Scotland.

He held pastorates in North and South Carolina for ten years, followed by two years as resident scholar for Chalcedon, during which time he was editor of the *Journal of Christian Reconstruction*. Since 1981 he has been at Reformed Theological Seminary in Jackson, Mississippi, where he is Professor of Systematic Theology and regularly teaches a Sunday school class at the First Presbyterian Church. He has written several books and numerous journal articles.

His wife, Caroline, holds a Bachelor of Arts and Master of Divinity degree from Edinburgh University. She teaches part-time in a local high school.

The Kellys have five children and live in Jackson, Mississippi.

The typeface for the text of this book is *Times Roman*. In 1930, typographer Stanley Morison joined the staff of *The Times* (London) to supervise design of a typeface for the reformatting of this renowned English daily. Morison had overseen type-library reforms at Cambridge University Press in 1925, but this new task would prove a formidable challenge despite a decade of experience in paleography, calligraphy, and typography. *Times New Roman* was credited as coming from Morison's original pencil renderings in the first years of the 1930s, but the typeface went through numerous changes under the scrutiny of a critical committee of dissatisfied *Times* staffers and editors. The resulting typeface, *Times Roman*, has been called the most used, most successful typeface of this century. The design is of enduring value to English and American printers and publishers, who choose the typeface for its readability and economy when run on today's high-speed presses.

Substantive Editing:
Michael S. Hyatt

Copy Editing:
Susan Kirby

Cover Design:
Steve Diggs & Friends
Nashbville, Tennessee

Page Composition:
Xerox Ventura Publisher
Printware 720 IQ Laser Printer

Printing and Binding:
Maple-Vail Book Manufacturing Group
Manchester, Pennsylvania

Cover Printing:
Strine Printing Company Inc.
York, Pennsylvania